Same Homework

NEW PLAN

How to Help Your _{Disorganized} Kid Sit Down and Get it Done

Disorganized

How to Help Your Kid Sit Down and Get it Done

SALLY G. HOYLE, PhD

Child & Family Press • Washington, DC

Child & Family Press is an imprint of the Child Welfare League of America. The Child Welfare League of America is the nation's oldest and largest membership-based child welfare organization. We are committed to engaging people everywhere in promoting the well-being of children, youth, and their families, and protecting every child from harm. All proceeds from the sale of this book support CWLA's programs in behalf of children and families.

CHILD WELFARE LEAGUE OF AMERICA, INC.
HEADQUARTERS
440 First Street, NW, Third Floor, Washington, DC 20001-2085
E-mail: books@cwla.org

CURRENT PRINTING (last digit)
10 9 8 7 6 5 4 3 2 1

Cover illustration by Jason Levinson
Cover and text design by Jennifer R. Geanakos
Edited by Tegan A. Culler

Printed in the United States of America

ISBN-13: 978-1-58760-073-9
ISBN-10: 1-58760-073-0

Library of Congress Cataloging-in-Publication Data
Hoyle, Sally G.
    Same homework, new plan : how to help your disorganized kid sit down and get it done / by Sally G. Hoyle.
        p. cm.
    Summary: "Presents tips and techniques to help parents teach their children ages 7–15 to manage homework better in the short term and become more organized, independent learners in the long term. Special emphasis on children whose homework problems are due to ADHD or executive function problems. Includes information on outside resources and working with schools and administrators"—Provided by publisher.
    Includes bibliographical references (p. 93).
    ISBN-13: 978-1-58760-073-9 (pbk. : alk. paper)
    ISBN-10: 1-58760-073-0 (pbk. : alk. paper)
    1. Homework. 2. Education—Parent participation. I. Title.

LB1048.H698 2005
371.3'028'1—dc22   2005015835

CONTENTS

To my homework team,
Chris, Steve, and John

CHAPTER 1

The Homework Wars

A t some time between four and seven o'clock, your children arrive home. The daily after-school dialogue goes like this:

You: "How was school?"

Kid (almost always): "Fine."

You: "Do you have homework?"

Kid (long pause): "Yes."

You throw dinner together and drop off one of the kids at soccer practice, hoping that the other's homework will be completed when you get back. When you come home, you find your child watching cartoons.

You: "Is the homework done?"

Kid (another long pause): "No."

You: "Well, why are you watching cartoons?"

Kid: "I just want to see the end of this one."

Fast forward to after supper. The homework still is not done. The screaming and crying begins. "You had all afternoon to do this!"

you shriek at your elementary-, middle- or high-school student. "What have you been doing?"

A few weeks later, the report card comes, and it isn't pretty. You yell and scream and make an appointment for a conference with the teacher, only to learn what you'd already guessed: that the grades would be better if your child would *just do the homework*. You feel like a bad parent, but the teacher doesn't understand what it is like to dig through that disaster of a bookbag and figure out what your child isn't doing. Plus, you *know* that your child is smart enough to do it on his own, so you start to get really angry about his laziness. He is grounded until the grades come up. The crying over homework doesn't end. It is like he is trying to pay you back for taking away TV time, and you are at the end of your rope.

Homework problems occur with startling frequency in families of children ages 7 to 16. If the kids are not doing their homework by age 16, most parents have given up. They have lost the homework war. But many parents do not realize that their children may not get their homework done because they have organizational problems. They are underachievers, and the problem is *not* laziness. Screaming and grounding them will not work. In fact, these parenting techniques that are successful in decreasing other problem behaviors can actually backfire if the underlying reasons for the homework problem are not known.

How do I know this? One of my sons struggled terribly with school, and homework was a nightmare. For much of elementary school, teachers considered him to be lazy or below average. We knew that he was bright and underachieving. Thus began a long journey involving psychological assessments, teacher meetings, tutors, and neurological assessment. It took three years to identify the problem, which turned out to be compromised executive function (more on this later), and about three more years to turn around the damage done by well-intentioned educators who were sure they knew our son better than we did. The problem was compounded by an extraordinary amount of homework and the long periods of time it took for him to complete it.

Homework's Heavy Toll on Families

As I write this, it is summer vacation, that time of the year when my sons smile more than usual because there is no homework. If your family has homework problems, you know what I am talking about: your children run around outside with friends, ride bikes, watch cartoons, and play video games. The tempers and tension and anxiety about homework are gone, replaced by age-appropriate concerns relating to sleepovers, movies, sports, trips to amusement parks and summer jobs.

Close your eyes for a moment and imagine your child in June or July (assuming your child isn't in summer school). Imagine how nice it would be if your child could be that happy and relaxed year round. And I bet you notice how much more relaxed *you* feel during this time of year. No checking homework, no whining, and no late nights. No more pencils, no more books, no more teachers' dirty looks, as the old rhyme goes—because homework has serious effects on parents' ability to cope, too.

Gone are the days when a parent can come home, relax, and enjoy a nutritious, homemade meal eaten while the family chats about the events of the day. All over the country, parents arrive home from work tired, feeling they've earned a little downtime, wishing only to hear the words, "I finished my homework." Instead, more often than not, they quiz kids on vocabulary words, help them with Internet or library research, or try to figure out math problems that don't look like the ones they learned many years ago.

Whose homework is it, after all? If parents have to supervise, get materials, and ensure that work is completed, isn't it *their* homework too? When I speak with groups of parents, I joke that I have been doing homework for almost 40 years: 20 years for my own education and the rest in supervising my children's education. Some parents even start their homework coaching by phone before they arrive home, increasing their stress level to a near frenzy by the time they walk in the door (Barnett & Gareis, 2004). Especially when you are deep in the homework trenches, you may be tempted to ask why you and your child are going through all this stress and frustration. What is homework good for?

Despite its negative points, homework does have its place. Educators and administrators use homework to fill a number of goals:

- to increase achievement

- to give students an opportunity to practice or review what was learned during the day

- to learn concepts that cannot be covered during the school day

- to communicate with parents on students' progress

- to teach students to develop study skills

- to teach self-discipline and build character

- to encourage children to see learning as something that occurs outside of the school context

Viewed from this perspective, the rationale for homework makes sense. Teachers do have our children's best interests at heart when they assign homework, and many teachers work hard to make homework timely and interesting. Yet the emphasis on homework in some schools has become extreme. This is what worries me as a psychologist. If homework takes almost all of their free time, when are children and teenagers supposed to have time to think, to imagine, to get bored, to meander about the neighborhood doing nothing? How are parents going to have time to pursue a hobby, get some exercise, and enjoy time with their kids free of homework nagging? Children learn things by playing and interacting with friends. If they are chained to a desk, they will miss experiences that can contribute positively to social and intellectual development. As Walker Percy so aptly said, "You can get all A's and still flunk life."

Perhaps the answer is that we all know that homework in and of itself is not bad for kids. It becomes bad when there is too much of it, or if you have a child who cannot do homework *at the speed the teacher estimates it will take.* It becomes bad when we skip family visits or a trip to the zoo because there is no time to do these things and complete the homework. And it is truly sad to see a young child with stress symptoms similar to that of an overworked adult, "burnt out" at the ripe old age of 9.

So in the face of this, what do we do? You can't change the work your child must complete for school, at least not overnight. You *can* go about it in a better way, looking for creative shortcuts and strategies to save time. You *can* see that your children don't feel badly about themselves because homework is hard for them. You *can* work smarter so that you are not screaming, "Just get it done!" and then left feeling like a bad parent. You do not have to let it disrupt your life and your family's life. Here are the tools that will help you and your children come up with your new plan for tackling homework.

For underachieving or disorganized kids and their parents, homework is a special challenge. Chapter 2 examines why some children underachieve and the emotional costs of these academic struggles. Although children may underachieve for a variety of reasons, I place a special emphasis on how executive function problems and Attention-Deficit/Hyperactivity Disorder (popularly known as ADHD) figure into homework.

Chapter 3 is devoted to various strategies that you and your child can use at home to formulate your own homework plan. I've included ways to get started and suggestions for approaching different types of assignments. Chapter 4 contains tips to help your student learn to organize himself, so that he can transfer these skills into adulthood. Chapter 5 contains ideas on low-tech and high-tech solutions that may help your child.

About this time, you may be thinking, "Okay, if there are ways I can help my child, it sure sounds like a lot of work and a lot of time for me." It is. But you don't need to try to do it all yourself. In Chapter 6, I discuss options and techniques for accessing help outside the home. I examine how to work with educators and the school to benefit your child and describe potentially helpful school and community programs and services. You might need help from a psychologist, social worker, or counselor along the way, and I make recommendations about when and how to involve these professionals.

The parent of the successful, disorganized child must work harder than other parents to encourage, monitor, and teach the student. For busy parents, providing this kind of support can be challenging. Chapter 7 offers ideas for parents as they manage the ups and downs of homework and helping a child get organized. "But I am disorganized myself," you might be thinking. "How can I help my child learn to organize anything?" We are not all born with organizational skills. Even if your home, office, or car is a mess, you can still help your child by learning some of organizational strategies I outline here. In this chapter, I also include recommendations for families with special challenges that affect the homework routine: divorced or single parents, grandparents raising grandchildren, parents or children with chronic illness, and so on.

Some parents are beginning to question the utility of homework, or at least the amounts of homework that children receive in some schools. I'll speak more in Chapter 8 about a community that made some changes to how its schools approach homework. If you feel that the amount of homework is excessive, you may want to work to modify your school's practices also. Finally, I offer video, Internet, and print resources that may help you in your homework journey.

Homework problems can be approached like any other stressful life experience: We can complain about it and let it pollute other parts of our lives, or we can develop a plan, preserve our sanity, and keep working at it until it gets better. Sometimes it takes time, effort, and money to get to the other side of the Homework Doldrums; sometimes all it takes is a few Post-it notes and an office supply or two. I sincerely hope that the material presented in this book will help your child become more successful in school, end tears over homework, and contribute to a positive parent-child relationship.

CHAPTER 2

The Causes and Costs of Underachievement

L et's start with what causes underachievement in the first place. If you don't figure out what is causing the problem, it will be harder to find solutions. Kids underachieve in school for numerous reasons; you are sometimes more likely to be aware of a problem than the teachers because you know your child best.

Power Struggles

Let's get one thing straight: If they have anything better to do, no student really wants to be doing homework, and no parent really wants to be supervising homework. A power struggle is implicit in the whole homework saga, and this may be part of the problem.

So how do you avoid the power struggle? First, admit that homework is not a thrill a minute for either of you. Let your child know that you realize many other things seem more interesting or important. It is okay to be sympathetic with your child. Yes, she has been sitting at a desk all day listening to the blah-blah-blah of teachers, eating cold Tater Tots, or getting teased on the bus. Acknowledge the stresses of your child's day. Without whining, it is all right to say that sometimes it is no picnic to be a parent, either, working all day inside or outside of the home (or both) and having to crack the whip to get the homework done. You get tired of being the Homework Bully.

Second, explain why it is important to you as a parent that your child does homework regardless of how you both sometimes feel about it: You want him to go to college; you want her to get a good job; you think that it will teach him a sense of responsibility so that when he is an adult he will pay his bills. Third, present the consequences if the homework is not completed. Then stick to your guidelines *consistently*. Parents of students with failing grades find remarkable improvement when they restrict computer time, video games, or cell phones until there is evidence of a favorable academic forecast. Finally, redirect your child into planning and problem-solving mode. Some suggestions on how to do this appear in Chapter 3.

If you've done all this and you are still fighting the homework wars, your child may be underachieving for another reason, such as those described in the remainder of this chapter.

Depression

Homework problems may be the result of undiagnosed depression in children. One symptom of depression in children and teenagers is loss of interest in usual activities. Another potential symptom is fatigue or lack of energy. A young person who is clinically depressed may have difficulty completing assignments. Look for the following symptoms:

- Depressed mood (or in children, irritable mood) most of the day, every day.

- Less interest in usual activities

- Sleeps too much or too little

- Moves too much or moves very slowly nearly every day

- Tired, lacks energy

- Feels worthless

- Trouble concentrating or making decisions

- Recurrent thoughts of death (American Psychiatric Association, 1994, p. 339)

If you think that your child may be depressed, schedule an evaluation with a mental health professional (psychologist, psychiatrist, social worker, or licensed counselor) as soon as possible.

Giftedness

You may be surprised to learn that gifted students can be under-achievers. Gifted students may not do assignments because the repetition of material they have already mastered easily is boring to them. They also may lose points for other reasons—for example, if they do not write down the steps in math computations, because they do it in their heads. They may develop an assignment in an elaborate, sophisticated way that doesn't meet the teacher's criteria.

Some people with giftedness and learning problems (e.g., gifted with ADHD or a learning disability) escape detection of teachers and parents. In my practice, I see many college students who have recently discovered that they have learning or attention problems. It is hard to imagine that a young person with a significant learning or attention problem could make it through 12 years of school without anyone knowing it, but it happens. Bright children find ways to compensate for their areas of difficulty, and these systems may not break down until they attend college.

If a gifted student is underachieving, the parent should consult with the gifted education personnel in the school system to develop strategies for managing routine assignments that do not interest the student. Or perhaps the teacher would be willing to accept credit for less repetition of a concept if the student produced something more involved on the same topic.

Executive Function Problems

My education in organizational problems started when my son was in preschool. His development was normal, but teachers said he was not learning school-related material well. At the time, we thought the teachers were being picky. I now know this was the first sign of a problem that would grow with time.

I am a licensed psychologist, specializing in work with children, adolescents, and their families for over 20 years. I have seen countless youngsters diagnosed with a learning disability or attention deficit disorder, but none of this prepared me for my son's difficulties. When I encounter a problem, I start doing research. I reviewed current literature on organizational functions of the brain, especially something called "executive function." I found out that an executive function problem is a deficit in information processing that affects organization, attention, and the travel of information in and out of the brain.

Dr. Martha Denckla, an expert in this area, calls executive functioning problems a "neuropsychological weakness originating in the frontal lobes or interconnected regions which results in impairments with academic and social consequences" (Denckla, 1996). In terms of school tasks, executive functioning affects the child's ability to listen, pay attention, memorize facts, take notes, write, take tests, learn to read, and other school tasks. Executive function, or executive dysfunction in my son's case, explained why he didn't know what he was supposed to do in school or on homework. Something as simple as learning a locker combination in middle school can be difficult for some children with executive dysfunction.

Dr. Russell Barkley, a psychologist who is an expert on ADHD, devotes a chapter in his book, *Attention Deficit Hyperactivity Disorder* (Barkley, 1998) to the concept of executive function. As Dr. Barkley explains it, from infancy, humans have to learn to manage their own responses to the world around them. We have to make decisions about when to respond, how to respond, and when to stop responding. From the time that you first play peek-a-boo with your baby, he or she is making complicated decisions about what to do. You play peek-a-boo, the baby smiles, then stops smiling until something amusing occurs again. Part of learning the art of what psychologists call "self-regulation" is figuring out when *not* to do things, when *not* to respond. This is called "behavioral inhibition," and it involves waiting to respond until one has a chance to think about the event or situation or until other elements in the environment no longer require so much attention. The millions of mini-decisions like this that we make all day are part of the "executive functions."

As children grow older, the decisionmaking becomes more complicated. For example, if you tell your child "no snacks before dinner" and she wants to eat cookies, she has to decide whether the immediate satisfaction of eating the cookies outweighs the punishment for breaking a rule. She also may consider whether she is likely to get more cookies if she waits until after dinner. Her friend may be visiting and suggest that they have a tea party using real cookies, thus creating a diversion that may interfere with the decision to follow the rule. The ability to think through scenarios like this one, to weigh the pros and cons of different courses of action, and to choose the best one, illustrates some of the processes involved in executive function.

Dr. Barkley describes four executive functions:

- Working memory: In the example about cookies before dinner, remembering, "Mom said 'No snacks before dinner.'"

- Internalization of speech. Talking to oneself mentally. "Though it would be fun to have a tea party with real cookies, Mom said no snacks and cookies are snacks. Plus I could get in trouble."

- Self-regulation of feelings and motivation: "I would feel really good if I had a cookie now, but I am not supposed to have it. If I am really hungry and ask Mom, she may let me have some fruit or carrots."

- Reconstitution: (After eating cookies) "Oh no! I wasn't supposed to do that! Mom's going to be mad."

If you can understand more about how your child thinks, it can help you to solve the problem. So how does disorganized thinking affect children's day-to-day functioning? Most parents require that the child be responsible for cleaning up his or her room. When my son was about 10, his room was a hodgepodge of game cards, Legos, school papers, music materials, office supplies, books, dirty clothes, and trash. If I were to mentally formulate a plan to clean his room, it might look something like this:

- Put Legos in plastic bin.

- Put game cards in baskets.

- Put baskets with game cards on a shelf.

- Sort school papers and throw some out.

- Put books in the bookcase.

- Put office supplies in the desk.

- Put dirty clothes in the hamper in the bathroom.

- Place miscellaneous toys in the bins in the closet.

My son formulated no such plan. He had no idea where to *start*. If I suggested strategies verbally, he became overwhelmed. If I wrote them down, he might follow the list but get frustrated and angry. I tried giving him a few tasks, returning a few minutes later to see if he could figure out what to do next, but as you have probably experienced if you are the parent of a disorganized child, he could get off track in a multitude of ways: he would start to put the Legos in the bin, notice a piece he'd been looking for to complete a vehicle, and start building something. Or he'd get to picking up the mess of game cards but decide to go find rubber bands to put around the card decks first; when he left his room, he'd see his brother playing a computer game, stop to watch, and forget about the room. Or he'd start sorting school papers but have no idea which ones to toss and which ones to keep, and start reading a report he wrote at the start of the year. He could not stay on track, and I wondered why.

About this time, you might be wondering what causes executive function problems. I wish I could tell you, but the cause is largely unknown. I tell kids and teenagers that it means that their brains work slightly differently than other kids, but it does not mean that they are dumb or stupid.

We do know that executive function problems often—but not always—go hand in hand with attention problems and learning disabilities. It can also be the case that a student has difficulty with executive function without any concurrent educational or attentional problem. This circumstance tends to occur in bright students identified as underachieving.

Learning Disabilities

If your child is underachieving, he or she may also have a learning disability. Most people are familiar with the term "dyslexia," a learning disorder where the child has severe trouble learning to read. A learning disability means that the child is not able to work to potential in a particular skill area due to impairments in cognitive processing.

The prevalence of children who have learning disabilities and concurrent executive dysfunction is not clear. According to Ellenberg

(1999), children with learning disabilities tend to have executive dysfunction in the area of disability only. For example, if the child had a reading disability, he or she may have trouble with verbal working memory, one of the executive functions. It is very common that individuals with specific learning disabilities also exhibit ADHD, and Ellenberg (1999) writes that it is highly likely that children with both learning disabilities and ADHD will have executive dysfunction. The only way to find out if your child has a learning disability is to see that he or she gets a battery of cognitive tests—usually administered by a school psychologist—that will tell what areas show a discrepancy between ability level and actual achievement.

ADHD

I have just had another one of those phone conferences where the teacher talks about how my client is a nice kid but he shows an inability to pay attention. I can tell by the tone in her voice that she is trying hard to like this boy, but he is driving her nuts. She observes that he is motivated to do well. She wonders if he "needs medication." He has Attention-Deficit/Hyperactivity Disorder or ADHD.

The ADHD Diagnosis

According the American Psychological Association, ADHD is "a persistent pattern of inattention and/or hyperactivity impulsivity that is more frequent and severe than is typically observed in individuals at a comparable level of development" (American Psychological Association, 1994). A diagnosis of ADHD refers to individuals who display symptoms of inattention for a period of at least six months. This can occur in the presence of hyperactivity (predominantly hyperactive-impulsive type), in the absence of hyperactivity (predominantly inattentive type), or with some of both inattention and hyperactivity (combined type). It used to be called ADD, or Attention Deficit Disorder, but the name and the definition of this disorder has evolved over time in the fields of psychiatry, psychology and education.

No single, definitive test for ADHD exists, but psychologists have many good measures for aiding in diagnosis, including interviews and parent questionnaires. In my opinion, the best kind of evaluation is a neuropsychological evaluation. A neuropsychologist is a psychologist who specializes in brain functioning. Although a neuropsychological assessment is time-consuming, it reveals important information on how your child thinks. If cost or insurance coverage or availability precludes neuropsychological assessment, a psychological assessment is the next best thing; school psychologists and licensed clinical psychologists can administer psychological assessments. Psychological assessment includes IQ testing and individual achievement testing. ADHD can also be diagnosed by pediatricians, psychiatrists, psychologists, and social workers who have training and experience working with children and adolescents. A trained professional can make a diagnosis through clinical observation and clinical interview.

Though ADHD appears to be a common problem, other psychological disorders can look like ADHD. For example, children who have been traumatized in some way (i.e. posttraumatic stress disorder) can display clinical symptoms similar to ADHD. Anxiety disorders can resemble ADHD, and unidentified giftedness can also appear to have the same symptoms as ADHD. (Webb, 2000). It is important that you obtain a thorough assessment by someone who has experience with clinical diagnosis.

Not all individuals with ADHD have deficits in executive function, but a high proportion of them have significant problems with planning and organization. Ellenberg (1999) recommends that children with ADHD have an assessment of the executive functions, which would be a neuropsychological assessment. Given the numbers of children thought to manifest attention problems and the availability of neuropsychologists, insurance coverage factors, and so forth, many children will not have such evaluations, however. In fact, most children that I see for clinical consultation or therapy and who are diagnosed with ADHD have had none of these evaluations. A neuropsychological evaluation is not required in order to address an attention problem.

What is ADHD like for Kids and Families?

My young clients with ADHD tell me that it seems like they have no control over what happens to them in school. They become used to getting in trouble, then getting out of trouble. At home, chores do not get done and they get grounded for bad report cards. Life becomes a series of efforts to avoid getting in trouble and appearing to be stupid. This explains the lying that some ADHD kids and teens engage in: getting in trouble gets old after a while, so they lie to avoid punishment. By the time they get to my office and someone has figured out why all of this is happening to them, it is usually a relief to have an explanation.

Youngsters with ADHD can be delightful, energetic, and funny. They think of novel ways to use materials and ask questions other children do not ask because their minds are always active. Many days, they seem like everyone else. But there is always something that requires a different approach for a parent and the "somethings" change as the child gets older. For example, contrast the challenges of providing safe supervision and teaching the alphabet to an overly active 4-year-old versus teaching an attention-challenged young person to drive a car or to keep track of his house keys and cell phone. The parent of a person with ADHD can be in a constant state of problem management. This can be exhausting depending on the severity of ADHD, concurrent learning disabilities or psychological problems, and family functioning.

Furthermore, organizational problems can affect the whole family. If there is constant yelling and conflict surrounding homework, this creates a very hostile home environment, and even the siblings that are completing homework and working up to potential are affected by the negative emotional atmosphere. Parental stress can exacerbate a bad situation. Marital problems can develop or worsen, and well-meaning relatives might start telling parents what to do. On the plus side, however, siblings of the child having homework trouble will learn to be good teachers. A spirit of cooperation can be established between parent and child. The student who experiences less difficulty can develop empathy for the sibling.

If you can have a sense of humor about your child's difficulties, this can help you to cope. One bright, achievement-oriented 9th grader with ADHD dutifully brought caulk to school because it was written in his planner. When the student handed the caulk to the teacher, the teacher expressed confusion, then smiled and said, "I asked you to bring in your *calcs*" (i.e., calculators)." This was a hilarious mistake that the teen was able to laugh about too. But we cannot always laugh off the ways that life is different for the disorganized young person, and it is helpful to know about emotional pitfalls discussed on page 21.

Medication

Medication for ADHD is prescribed by physicians (typically pediatricians, psychiatrists, or family physicians) and in some states psychologists. Numerous online and print resources about medication exist, including Russell A. Barkley's *Taking Charge of ADHD* (Barkley, 2000) and the National Institutes of Mental Health website (www.nimh.gov). Bear in mind that medications change every few years as new research comes out.

Medication does not eliminate executive dysfunction or ADHD. That being said, considering medication that could reduce a student's disorganization is a tough decision for parents. After all, it is possible to manage ADHD without medication if one has a highly structured school and home program with behavioral management components. If you answer *yes* to the following questions, however, you may want to consider medication:

- Has your entire family been affected by the attention problem to an extent where there is constant conflict?

- Have you done all the "right" parenting things—made efforts to increase your child's self-esteem, taken him/her to therapy, had psychological testing to confirm the diagnosis—but nothing seems to work?

- Has your child's attention problem placed him/her at risk for harm or is he/she hurting others?

- Has your child experienced chronic school failure?

On the other hand, if you agree with the following statements, you probably should *not* consider medication until you have a formal assessment by a trained mental health professional:

- The teacher says to put the child on medication, but you have had no assessments with a pediatrician or mental health professional.

- Your family is going through a period of severe stress.

- Your child has experienced many medical problems.

- You are not sure whether or not your child has an attention problem.

- Your child seems unusually bright or talented and IQ has not been assessed.

To treat executive function and ADHD, practitioners typically recommend a combination of therapies, and often, medication. Behavioral therapy, a common approach to treating the direct issues that ADHD and executive dysfunction present, usually involves six to eight sessions with the parents, the child, and a licensed psychologist or other trained mental health practitioner. It is covered under many insurance plans. Some parents (and some children) are reluctant to try medication, and in such cases, behavioral therapy alone may be the best option for managing these conditions.

For parents who do wish to include medication in their child's treatment, psychiatrists and pediatricians may recommend that behavioral therapy begin before starting any medications, or begin when the medication trial begins, or be ongoing. I have found it effective for many children with executive dysfunction and ADHD to have an initial period of therapy and then come in for brief therapy as problems arise. Finally, in some geographical areas, "organizational tutoring" or "executive function coaching," may be available. These services involve teaching the client organizational skills similar to those discussed in the rest of this book. Because these services are educational in nature, most health insurance plans do not cover them.

Emotional Factors and Underachievement

A child told me recently that his teacher is mad at him all day. At an age when the child should be *less* dependent on adult help, the child who requests constant assistance from parents or teachers is *more* dependent on these adults. Parents and teachers may feel frustrated or overburdened by the constant demands of the underachieving or disorganized student. School is structured so that grades are rarely private. Underachieving children wonder why their friend gets the "A" and they get the "D," because they are just as smart. It hurts to be teased by other kids when they ask questions about what the teacher just said. So it is not surprising that a variety of emotional problems can develop. Let's examine more closely the emotional price of underachievement.

Low Self-Esteem

Underachievers often have low self-esteem. One second grader with ADHD left the following note (grammar and spelling left unchanged) for his parent: "Der dad, I am sory for not lisning to you I need to do difreuntly nexse time." Another student wrote in an end-of-first-grade introduction letter to the new second-grade teacher, "I have problems wit caching up on werc." Apparently, this student felt that she should warn the teacher of the trouble keeping up with the class before she met her.

When I see organizationally challenged children in my office, some argue with me about how dumb they are. They are convinced that they are stupid. I am convinced that they are not. Almost every day, they are faced with some kind of failure. Parents may be doing all the "right" things to foster positive self-esteem, but if the child is faced with daily confirmation that she doesn't measure up, all the good parenting in the world may be ineffective in raising self-esteem. The antidote to low self-esteem is a supportive school and home environment where the child experiences success at some things.

Depression

I wrote earlier about how kids with undiagnosed depression could have homework problems. Here, I am talking about depression caused by chronic stress and failure relating to underachievement. Children and teenagers who are up late doing assignments have no free time. This makes for a bad combination with constant pressure to perform better, or faster, leaving some students depressed. Should this come as a surprise to anyone? Even in elementary school, the pressures are enormous. There are "challenge words" "ultra-super challenge words" and "magnificent, unbelievable challenge words." (Okay, I made some of that up, but you know what I am talking about.) The student with executive dysfunction experiences a cycle of working hard with results (i.e., grades) that do not match the effort.

Anxiety

It makes me anxious just thinking about standardized test time at school. In some school systems, teachers are pressured to produce students who will get high scores and make the school look good. Most parents report that when state proficiency tests are given, the teachers seem to whip children into an emotional frenzy preparing for the tests. Unwittingly, the No Child Left Behind legislation has placed more stress on schools and thus on our children. Psychologists see many children for anxiety problems, some of which come from school pressures such as these.

Some children have specific anxiety concerns like math anxiety, "a learned emotional response" (www.mathacademy.com). There exists a perception that no normal person would be good at math. Math teachers and mathematicians have long been viewed as geeks. Think about your own stereotypes about math. If you think that your child has math anxiety, visit the website or ask someone to print off a copy of the article at http://www.mathacademy.com/pr/minitext/anxiety/index.asp for you. It contains specific strategies for math anxiety.

School Phobia

School phobia is a type of anxiety disorder wherein the child refuses to go to school due to anxiety. This problem usually requires behavioral treatment by a psychologist or counselor. Organizational problems have not been connected with school phobias in the research literature, but a child who has chronic school failure and undiagnosed attention or learning problems can manifest school phobia.

Bus Refusal

Bus refusal can become a problem with children who have high levels of stress relating to homework. The child may beg the parent for a ride because the child cannot manage the normal stresses of the school bus—the teasing, name-calling, and aggression that occurs on buses with some regularity. Bus refusal can also be a sign that discipline on the bus is needed (i.e. bullying is a factor), that the child is experiencing separation anxiety, or any number of other problems as well.

Low Frustration Tolerance

Frustration at high levels for long periods of time, and low levels of positive reinforcement, result in low self-esteem as well as low frustration tolerance. The result is that the child loses the ability to bounce back after stressful life events. It is no small wonder that kids cannot tolerate things going wrong, whether it be losing something small or a tough homework assignment. I see children in therapy who are referred because they cry when they can't find their shoes or understand a math concept. They are under high stress and are living in a world where results are expected quickly.

Anger Management

Once, as I was waiting in a doctor's office, a lady told me that she waited four hours one day. When she complained to the doctor, the doctor referred her to a psychologist for anger management. Now, who wouldn't be angry if they waited four hours for a doctor's appointment? Similarly, the student with 2 to 3 hours of homework every night, who is ill-treated by peers and teachers, is angry. Managing anger also involves good problem-solving skills that a person with an executive function problem may not possess. At 9 P.M., with homework incomplete, many parents no longer demonstrate good anger management either.

Clinical Signs of Stress

School can be an extremely high-pressure environment for a child. In some high schools, there is extraordinary pressure to take a large number of Advanced Placement and Honors courses. Parents buy into it by bragging about how many such courses the child takes. Advertisers have had their hand in this "Be The Best" mania, too: I recently received a mailing from a national test preparation company that said, "Is your child's score high enough?" It went on to discourage parents from settling for second best. Chances are, if your child is having a lot of trouble in school, he or she is evidencing signs of stress. In children and teenagers, stress is manifested in the following ways:

- Somatic complaints like headaches or stomachaches

- Sleep problems

- Decreased peer interaction or poor peer relationships

- Acting like a younger child

- Oppositional behavior or "bad attitude"

- Eating problems

- Insecurity

- Depression

- Excessive dependency on television, video games, or computer

- Aggression towards others

The Meltdown

If you are reading this book, you are no stranger to the meltdown. It is a test of the emergency homework system. Your child flunks the spelling pretest, comes home, and dissolves into tears. Or there is a book report/science project/test coming up and your child becomes easily overwhelmed by the task demands. All parents respond differently to the meltdown, but one thing that is really important is to figure out what to do so it doesn't get worse. When a homework emergency is in progress, the right strategy can shorten or eliminate it. In the next chapter, I will discuss strategies that will get you through your child's next meltdown.

When Should a Parent Seek Professional Help?

If your child is experiencing emotional difficulty, it can be time to get professional help. As a general rule of thumb consider whether your child/family has sufficient support resources to manage the level of stress the child is experiencing? Are the problems to the point where you feel like you have run out of ideas? Do you feel like you are going to lose your temper daily? If so, you may want to look for help from a mental health professional or school counselor (see Chapter 6 for how to find a qualified professional).

If you feel like you have things under control, but you are frustrated, have a frank, supportive talk with your son or daughter about how difficult homework time is for the whole family. You might also try the homework feelings game described on page 42; the game cards allow the players to verbalize feelings about homework.

Let's Get to Work!

After many years of employing the techniques that will be described in this book, my son is an Honor Roll student, feels good about himself, and works independently needing minimal support. We have learned to laugh about the comical aspects of his problem like his spelling mistakes ("Pencilvainia"). And, he cleans his own room without assistance and does a terrific job. It will be hard work, and it may take a long time to get results; I will be honest about that. But it starts with identifying and accepting the problem, analyzing your child's situation, and finding things that work for your son or daughter. You can do this for your child. So let's get to work.

CHAPTER 3

Homework According to Hoyle

Short-Term Solutions for Tonight

N ow it is time to create a Homework Plan to flesh out strategies that will work for your underachieving child. The Homework Plan will help you structure—and eventually to teach your child to structure—time and mental resources in order to get everything done. Your ultimate goal is to teach your child to manage homework better on her own so that things go smoothly in your family (more on how to get to that point in the next chapter), but for now, your primary goal is to make tonight better than last night and tomorrow night better than tonight.

Because it will depend on how much your child has to do and how much support or supervision she needs to complete the homework, your Homework Plan may not be the same every day. Your Homework Plan will also probably evolve over time. Nevertheless, part of creating a Homework Plan is finding the basic approaches that work for you and your child—and helping your child learn to apply a variety of tools in various contexts.

Routines of Homework Coaching

Although it's your child's homework, not yours, if you have a disorganized child, you will be the defining force in creating a Homework Plan that will work. Chapter 7 is entirely dedicated to strategies for coaches, but in the beginning, especially if you have a younger child, you'll need to help your child by taking on the specific tasks outlined below. Your eventual goal is to be able to turn these responsibilities over to your student, but this may not happen until his or her teenage years.

Keeping Up

You may not be able to keep track of assignments every day, and even the most disorganized youngster has days where they can sit down and get it done with minimal help. But the more you know about what is going on in school for each child, the better you will do at homework coaching. When you have time, read the assignment sheet, wade through the binder and/or backpack, read the notes the teacher sends home. Check the school's website (if there is one) to see if your child's teacher posts homework assignments. Some schools have phone "homework hotlines" for checking assignments. E-mail or call the teacher to get a status report. Many teachers have e-mail, and their grade sheets are on their computer, so it is not time-consuming to send you that information if you need it. In short, do the research.

Homework Supplies

Although low-tech and high-tech homework aids will be discussed Chapter 5, some things are pretty basic. It is your responsibility as homework coach to maintain supplies of pencils, pens, markers, notebook paper, colored pencils, markers or crayons (depends on the grade of the child) and graph paper. Get some self-adhesive notes like Post-it notes or flags. Have your child stick them on the paper when the teacher passes out the assignment. This provides a visual reminder to do it and to pass it back in the next day. You can also use self-adhesive notes to mark pages in a book that will be needed for an assignment. For example, when your student reads a social studies chapter, have him put a note on each page where there is a definition in bold print that will be needed for definitions on the homework. Highlighters can help some kids to identify key information and to stay on task, but check your school's policy on writing in books first.

Check on Follow Through

It is also your job to make sure students stick to the plans you devise together. At my house, the kids need a break after school, but if I don't hear papers rustling and backpacks being unzipped by 4 P.M., then I rally the team. If I am working, I call at about 3:00 to check in about homework status. On my work days, their father usually calls later in the afternoon to ascertain whether homework or video games are in progress. If it is video games, then he can try to get the video gamer back on track, thus avoiding annoyance when he walks in the door.

Binder and Backpack Management 101

If your student is disorganized, the binder/notebook/trapper containing his academic life may consist of a hodgepodge of notebook paper, worksheets, study guides, and junk. This binder is placed in a backpack or bookbag stuffed with more papers, gym clothes, a jacket, and who knows what else. Every week or two, try to help your student to sort out the mess. Make three piles: stuff to toss; stuff to keep in the binder; and stuff to keep in a pile in your child's room in case it is needed later for a notebook check. Please do not expect your child to do this on his or her own. If you are reading this book, he or she needs help.

Formulating the Homework Plan

The homework plan depends your child's age, ability level, work style, and your family's schedule. You'll probably find that it will evolve over time, as your family's activities shift and your child learns to manage the homework on his own.

In Homework Diagnostic #1, (see p. 31) I have developed a homework troubleshooter to help you and your young person get started on creating your Homework Plan. This is how the homework troubleshooter works: look at the left-hand column where it says, "Homework Problem," and identify what area (or areas) challenge your child or teenager. Then use the right-hand column, labeled "What to try," to get ideas for potential solutions. (During the rest of the chapter I describe the strategies that are offered here as solutions.) If a suggestion sounds like it will not work for some reason, try another. Please note: with each of these problems/strategies, I am assuming that you are in communication with the teacher and other routines of homework coaching as described in the previous section.

Diffusing Power Struggles

If homework drama has become routine in your family, part of the problem may be the power struggles I mentioned in Chapter 2. Address these struggles as described in Chapter 2, but expect that on bad days or in the days following a very tough homework night, your child may resist homework. When this happens, allow your child to vent about his or her day briefly. Open the complaint department for a short period of time, comment on the rigors of your child's day in a way that validates her concerns, such as, "I'm sorry that they are teaching ballroom dancing in gym." Then make a comment that switches gears to planning mode. (By the way, this can be done in person or via phone or e-mail if you work outside the home.) Here are a few ideas:

- "Why don't you take a break, then hit the books?"

- "Wow, sounds like a bad day. What is your plan to regroup so you can get your homework done?"

- "It's tough to have to work on that project when it is so nice outside. How do you think you could enjoy the weather and get your work done efficiently?"

HOMEWORK DIAGNOSTIC #1: Hoyle's Homework Troubleshooter

Homework Problem	What to Try:
Student does not do homework	Check for learning/attention problem Homework tracking sheet Use visual reminders Cut down extracurricular activities
Student lies about homework	Check school website or homework hotline Homework tracking sheet Develop goal-setting skills
Student hides homework	Same strategies as for lying about homework
Student does not write down all assignments	Work with teacher to develop strategy for copying assignments Teach student to use assignment book
Student does homework and loses it	Binder and bookbag management Put in same place daily Use Post-it notes or flags Have student leave notes for self on bathroom mirror Fax homework to teacher
Student forgets textbooks	Develop Daily Book Checklist Get duplicate set of books for home Establish network of peers in same classes to borrow books
Student procrastinates	Develop positive reinforcers Estimate time needed for each assignment Also estimate free time for the day Cut down extracurricular activities
Student has sloppy penmanship	Check fine motor coordination Check processing speed Sit at table or desk instead of couch, armchair, or floor

HOMEWORK DIAGNOSTIC #1: Hoyle's Homework Troubleshooter (continued)

Homework Problem	What to Try:
Student rushes homework	Teach student to check own work
	Use highlighter to slow pace
	Set limits about TV, computer time, etc.
	Start homework earlier
Student doesn't understand assignments once he is home	Obtain psychological assessment
	Use home reference materials
	Use Internet resources
	Consider tutoring
	Read instructions aloud
	Enroll in Homework Club
Student takes long periods of time to complete homework	Obtain psychological assessment
	Build in fun breaks
Student does poorly on tests	Make flashcards
	Use homework games
	Teach mnemonic and other strategies
Student has difficulty maintaining attention	Encourage student to talk self through problems
	Provide a reduced-stimulus environment
	Play music with no words as sound screen
	Earplugs, headphones, or fan
Student complains about homework	Focus on homework plan
	Create and play Homework Feelings Game
	Acknowledge difficulty
Student won't do homework without adult	Build independence in other areas
Student dislikes reading	Ask teacher to check reading ability
	Let child select nontraditional reading materials (cartoons, sports)
	Read aloud to your child
Student cries about homework	Ask student to go to room and calm down
	Break assignments into doable parts
	Teach child to positively reinforce self

- "I had a bad day too. I think I will take a break, and then check in with you on your homework."

- "You have a soccer game at 6 P.M. How can you get your homework done before you go so that you can relax and focus on the game?"

- "Gosh, your favorite TV shows are on tonight. What is the best way to get your work done before you watch them?"

- "Before we go to our religious service tonight, we all have a lot to get done. Let's figure out how to get it done so we have a plan for the afternoon."

Also have a frank discussion with your child about homework pitfalls like too much computer use for social or surfing purposes, or too much TV, too many phone calls, and time wasted by crying and carrying on about homework.

Create an Agenda

So now you and your student are ready to look at what your afternoon and evening will bring. The first thing I suggest families do when the child is ready to start homework is to look at the planner/assignment book and go over what needs to be completed that day, what the deadlines are for other assignments, and what the long-term projects are. Then the parent and child develop a plan of attack for that day. For parents who work, you can do this via phone when you call to check in with kids who are old enough to stay at home alone.

- Start out by looking at your child's planner or agenda or binder or homework folder with your child. If your child does not have a place to record homework assignments, create one on the computer or buy one. Ignore misspelled words or shorthand in the recording of assignments for now. You have bigger fish to fry.

- If there is more than one assignment, ask your child to decide what to do first. If there are numerous assignments, I think it works well to write a number next to each assignment, indicating the order in which the student will do it.

- Estimate, with your child, how long it will take to do each assignment. You can write this number next to the one signifying the order or completion. (i.e. "Write definitions for 20 spelling words, #1, 30 minutes.")

- Now, figure in what the family has scheduled for the day. Is there a violin lesson at 4 P.M.? Do you have to visit someone in the hospital? If you are at work, executing the Homework Plan by phone, should the student save things he/she needs help on for after you get home? Or after supper?

- Related to this, think about how much supervision/monitoring or homework coaching your student will need for each assignment. How can you juggle that with fixing supper, taking kids places, running an errand, etc.? Generally speaking, the younger your child, the more available you need to be for homework. Also, if grades are low or the family is under a lot of stress, your child will probably need more homework coaching.

- Summarize the plan for the day in a positive tone of voice. For example, "So, it looks like you will do your math and language arts, shoot hoops for a few minutes, then take your social studies notes. By then, I will have time to quiz you on your French vocabulary if you would like."

Establish a Homework Routine and a Study Environment

Most homework books say that the student should have a quiet, well-lit study space. This environment may not be compatible with your son or daughter's work style or the available environment. Parents are great at figuring out what works for their own children, however. You can use Homework Diagnostics #2 (see p. 36) to help you fine-tune your child's homework routine.

Remember that the environment can be made up of lots of elements besides the physical space. Visual, auditory, and tactile (touch) cues can all help indicate to a student that it is time to work. For example, when I was in graduate school, the time when I had the most academic work in my life, I had a study routine that went something like this: put on sweats, spread out books/papers, sharpen pencils, make a pot of coffee, listen to classical music. One student I know puts his pajamas (tactile) on as soon as he gets home when it is a heavy homework night. Another student likes to be by a window (visual) to study. Some kids need quiet, others a low level of noise (auditory). One child with test anxiety had a study routine involving silky sports pants and a citrus hand cream.

It may also be useful to establish "Homework Zones" and "No Homework Zones." Make it clear where your student should work. It may vary depending on the type of assignment. Sometimes my boys like to work together at the kitchen table, but if one of them has a lot to do, he heads to a desk in a quieter place and closes the door. Television, video games, and similar stimuli are not allowed in the Homework Zone. Along with Homework Zones, you may want to establish "Homework Time." Tailor this to the rhythms of your household and your child's work needs. Identify the blocks of time that your child has for work versus other activities. Is it the same time daily? Does it vary depending on family schedule? Are there breaks built in, or are they contingent on how much work there is, your child's progress, or other factors?

As part of creating a study environment, it can really help to develop a home resource library, if you can afford to do so. In the References section, I have a list of sample books that your library might contain, but at the very minimum, a dictionary, thesaurus, and atlas are a good start. You can also download information from the Internet and make folders for different topics.

HOMEWORK DIAGNOSTIC #2: Study Environment

Go over this list with your child and check the items that apply. What combination of items is optimal for getting homework done? Your student may check more than one item in each section, depending on the assignment.

Noise Level

- ❏ No distractions at all
- ❏ Very quiet
- ❏ Some background noise
- ❏ Loud background noise
- ❏ Homework with music playing

Social Support

- ❏ Work with other people around
- ❏ Work alone
- ❏ Homework with a friend
- ❏ Parent/homework coach in the room
- ❏ Parent/homework coach available by phone

Time Management

- ❏ Taking many short breaks
- ❏ Taking no breaks
- ❏ Taking one long break halfway through
- ❏ Homework immediately after school
- ❏ Homework after supper
- ❏ Homework in the car
- ❏ Homework during study hall

Positive Attitude

- ❏ Drink beverage while doing homework
- ❏ Wear comfortable clothing during homework
- ❏ Eat while doing homework
- ❏ Look out window while doing homework

Strategies for Homework Success

Okay, so now you have gotten your student started on a homework plan. What else do you need to know to make a dent in this problem? Part of both a short-term and long-term solution to homework trouble is having at your disposal a grab bag of techniques that will help your child to learn. Don't feel like you should try all of these at once. Pick the one or two that you think will work, and when you feel stuck at some future time, pull out the book and switch to another. This helps to maintain your interest as well your student's.

Lists and Tracking Tools

To-Do Lists

Teach your child to develop some system of making lists when needed. Some kids need to keep several lists (or one list with several categories): *Today*, *This Week*, and *This Month* or *Long-Term* (like a project). Some kids do better keeping this list on paper, others on the computer. What you want your child to avoid is a bunch of little pieces of paper that will get lost.

The Daily Book Checklist

For the child who gets home and never has the right books, this may do it. Make a list of all the books and notebooks the student uses in school. For example:

- ❏ English Grammar book
- ❏ Reading book
- ❏ Science book
- ❏ Science notebook
- ❏ Social Studies book
- ❏ Social Studies folder
- ❏ Math book
- ❏ Gym clothes

- ❏ Clarinet
- ❏ Lunch money/ticket
- ❏ Homework packet

You can make copies of this list and ask your student to check off what he or she needs each day. Notice that I added other items that kids tend to forget, like gym clothes and an instrument. Feel free to tailor this to your child's daily needs.

The Homework Tracking Sheet

Ask your child's teacher or guidance counselor what the school uses in circumstances where parents need daily or weekly progress reports on the child's homework and schoolwork in general. Usually, these progress reports contain a list of each of the student's assignments by class. The teacher initials the report each day to ensure that the student has the correct assignment, then the parent initials the report to show that he or she has read the homework sheet. This approach saves you from the big surprise at report card time. This can also be done via e-mail if it is convenient for parent and teacher.

Get Creative!

You and your student can make studying fun by getting creative with material that must be memorized.

- **Sing a song:** Come up with a song or rap about the material you want to remember.

- **Mnemonic devices:** Use mnemonic devices, memory tools involving using familiar or silly information to remember harder information. For example, a mnemonic device for remembering the order of taxonomy and classification in science: King Phillip Came Over From Geneva, Switzerland (Kingdom, Phylum, Class, Order, Family, Genus, Species).

- **A picture is worth a thousand words:** You can also make a picture out of the material to be remembered. For example, remembering that Columbus arrived in America in 1492 by drawing a boat with 1492 on the sail. You can draw a timeline or flow chart to remember a difficult concept.

- **Get silly:** Make up silly sentences to study English grammar or a foreign language. My son used to struggle with grammar, and we would make up sentences like, (for compound verb), "Bob farted and belched after he ate a Kids Meal."

- **Produce a homework game show:** For example, we played "Name That Conquistador" in a manner imitating a popular game show to prepare for a social studies test.

- **Make a homework study game:** On a piece of posterboard or recycled cardboard, have your child draw a game board in the shape of a spiral, zigzag, or geometric pattern. Ask your child to draw it first in pencil, then trace it with magic marker or crayon. Label the "Start" and "Finish." To make it fun, let your student decorate the board, use stickers, and add spaces for things like "lose a turn" or "go ahead 3 spaces." Draw a box on the game board for the cards, which can be flashcards you have made or purchased on any subject. Find a pair of dice from another game, make some simple rules, and play. *How To Help Your Child With Homework* (Radencich & Schamm, 1996) offers additional study games on pages 137-146.

- **Give a lecture:** Have your child go over the material for the test, then give a lecture to you or to a pretend audience on the topic. They can use visual aids from the book or class assignments.

- **Make a word search:** For the weekly spelling tests, I love the puzzlemaker feature on www.school.discovery.com. All you do is type in the words, and it makes a word search for you.

- **Box of homework fun:** Keep a box labeled "Creative Ideas" with each of the strategies above (sing a song, get silly, homework game, and so on) written on an index card. When it's time to study for a test, have your child choose a card for study the activity of his or her choice.

Relaxation and Breaks

When homework is a stressful experience, soothing moments and breaks can be important for helping your child stay positive and on task. If it isn't too distracting for your student, music can be very calming and help improve your student's attitude. If your child is very tense, you may benefit from learning relaxation techniques from a book (try *A Boy and A Bear: The Children's Relaxation Book* [Lite, 1996]) or counselor. Even simple techniques such as a few minutes of deep breathing can relax an anxious child. Engaging in physical activities can be very relaxing as well. Make sure that your child is getting enough exercise, or do some kind of physical activity at home. Provided the child gets proper instruction, exercise balls or free weights can be a nice break.

Some kids can stay on track better if they take breaks. I find that most parents have a good handle on whether their child can manage breaks or not. If I suggest taking a few short breaks, many parents will say, "No, he'll never get back to work." Try to notice which type of break-taking works for your child. If you do think breaks will work for your child, and you'd like to make them rewarding, here are a few ideas:

- Go outside for 15-30 minutes

- Watch one cartoon

- Send five e-mails or Instant Messages

- Listen to five songs

- Make an obstacle course inside or outside of home

- Sing a song involving hand motions at top speed

- Dance wildly to your favorite song

- Tell jokes

If your child has trouble staying focused between breaks, practice quiet fidgeting with him or her. For some reason, fidgeting has gotten a bad reputation. I don't know about you, but when I am in a boring meeting, I move my feet, look for something in my purse, or if I am really bored, twiddle my thumbs (My father taught us to twiddle our thumbs so we would sit quietly in church). Why do we expect children to never fidget, especially kids with ADHD? Fidgeting quietly can help us to maintain attention. What are some good, non-disruptive things to fidget with? Your child could put something in his pocket that has a nice texture or is smooth (like a small stone), play with his pencil grip, clench and unclench his fists, twiddle his thumbs, squeeze his hands together, play a mental game (like counting something in the room), or manipulate a piece of jewelry, a hair tie, or a rubber band.

Reinforce the Right Behavior

Parents can build positive reinforcement into the homework routine in many ways. If you are out of ideas, try the Homework Card on page 44. It looks like frequent buyer card that adults get at restaurants; if we save the cards and have the restaurant check off our visits or cups of coffee, we get a free one. For the Homework Card, the student checks off a box on card, either for every day that homework is completed, or for every assignment, depending on the parent's wishes. The parent offers some extra privilege or something special when each card is completed. Some parents offer a trip to spend a dollar at a dollar store, for example. But the reward does not have to be something you buy for the child; it could be as varied as a game of CandyLand, staying up an extra hour, or picking what the family will have for supper. It depends what fits in with your parenting approach and what motivates your child.

Keep in mind that the best motivation for academic work is what psychologists call "intrinsic motivation," which means the student is motivated to learn because it makes her feel good, not just to please others. Avoid overpraising your child for things she should be doing anyway.

Damage Control

When we are having a horrible homework day at our house, everyone's problem-solving skills usually fly out the window. I developed a Homework Meltdown Kit, which is a plastic bag of inexpensive stuff that can be used on one of those nightmare homework days. It includes things to squeeze, like a Koosh ball, a foam ball, a huge pompon from the craft store, a stress ball, or a small container of Play Dough; something to fidget with, like those stretchy gel toys; gum or chewy candy to chew on; a ring pop (your student can work and lick at the same time); something to blow off steam, like a small container of bubbles or party favor blowouts; and a new office supply, like an interesting mechanical pencil or pen. These props can help your child to calm him or herself down on a particularly bad day. This is a way to restore a rational, problem-solving approach to homework.

The homemade Homework Feelings Game can be useful for venting feelings about school and homework on a bad day. It allows both the child and the parent to express feelings about homework coaching. Make a game board as described for the homework studying game on page 39, but this time, photocopy and cut out the Homework Feelings Cards on pages 45–50. I like to play where each person has to read and answer a homework feelings card each turn.

After each player rolls the dice and moves, he or she must pick a Homework Feelings Card, read it out loud, and answer questions aloud such as, "I feel smart when…" I have included cards for the kids and as well as for the adult or homework coach playing with the child. The adult items are things like, "Going to the parent-teacher conference is…" The game has no right or wrong answers, and each player advances the number they've rolled on the dice once they are done answering.

As you ease into your Homework Plan, you'll find that you use the Damage Control techniques less and less. You eventual goal is to cultivate an independent, organized learner working to his or her full ability (hopefully well before your child's high school graduation!) The techniques outlined in the next chapter will help you move into the next phase of the Homework Plan and encourage your child to adopt that role.

Homework Cards

Homework Card	Homework Card
❑ ❑ ❑ ❑ ❑	❑ ❑ ❑ ❑ ❑
❑ ❑ ❑ ❑ ❑	❑ ❑ ❑ ❑ ❑
❑ ❑ ❑ ❑ ❑	❑ ❑ ❑ ❑ ❑
❑ ❑ ❑ ❑ ❑	❑ ❑ ❑ ❑ ❑
Homework Card	Homework Card
❑ ❑ ❑ ❑ ❑	❑ ❑ ❑ ❑ ❑
❑ ❑ ❑ ❑ ❑	❑ ❑ ❑ ❑ ❑
❑ ❑ ❑ ❑ ❑	❑ ❑ ❑ ❑ ❑
❑ ❑ ❑ ❑ ❑	❑ ❑ ❑ ❑ ❑
Homework Card	Homework Card
❑ ❑ ❑ ❑ ❑	❑ ❑ ❑ ❑ ❑
❑ ❑ ❑ ❑ ❑	❑ ❑ ❑ ❑ ❑
❑ ❑ ❑ ❑ ❑	❑ ❑ ❑ ❑ ❑
❑ ❑ ❑ ❑ ❑	❑ ❑ ❑ ❑ ❑
-Homework Card	Homework Card
❑ ❑ ❑ ❑ ❑	❑ ❑ ❑ ❑ ❑
❑ ❑ ❑ ❑ ❑	❑ ❑ ❑ ❑ ❑
❑ ❑ ❑ ❑ ❑	❑ ❑ ❑ ❑ ❑
❑ ❑ ❑ ❑ ❑	❑ ❑ ❑ ❑ ❑

Homework Feelings Cards: Kids

Thinking about school makes me feel...	*When I am upset about school I...*
The best thing that ever happened to me in school was...	*When mom or dad yells at me about homework it is...*
I feel smart when...	*The thing my parents don't understand about homework is...*
I am bored when...	*When it is late and I'm still doing homework I am...*
When my brother or sister has less homework I am...	*The teacher always says I am...*

Homework Feelings Cards: Kids (cont.)

You have too much homework . What should you do?	*The best thing that ever happened to me in school was...*
I think best when...	*My teacher thinks I can...*
My favorite thing about school is...	*I am so sick of homework that I could...*
If I get a bad grade, the best thing to do is...	*It's not fair that I get so much homework so I...*
The worst thing that ever happened in school was...	*When my sister or brother says I am stupid, I...*

Homework Feelings Cards: Kids (cont.)

I would like to learn to . . .	*The worst thing that ever happened in school was. . .*
You have too much homework . What should you do?	*I would be better at homework if I. . . .*
I think best when. . .	*If I could be principal for a day I would. . .*
My favorite thing about school is. . .	*Listening to the teacher is. . . . .*
If I get a bad grade, the best thing to do is. . .	*I am bored when. . .*

Homework Feelings Cards: Kids (cont.)

My friends at school think I am...	*The teacher always says I am...*
When I am upset about school I.....	*I should get an award for...*
When mom or dad yells at me about homework it is...	*I feel smart when...*
The thing my parents don't understand about homework is...	*I feel happiest at school when...*
When it is late and I'm still doing homework I am...	*If I could be teacher for a day I would...*

Homework Feelings Cards: Coach

Thinking about my child's homework makes me feel...	*The thing my children don't understand about homework is...*
I know my child is smart when...	*When it is late and I'm still supervising homework I am...*
When one child has less homework than the others, I find...	*When I talk to my child's teacher I feel...*
When I am upset about how homework is going I...	*When the report card comes, I...*
When I am yelling at the kids about homework it is...	*I think my child would like school better if he/she would...*

Homework Feelings Cards: Coach (cont.)

If my child gets a bad grade, the thing to do is...	Going to open house at school is...
My child's teacher thinks I am...	I would like my child to learn...
I am so sick of homework that I could...	If I could change something about homework it would be...
When my child says he or she is stupid, I...	When I was in school, homework was...
Going to parent-teacher conference is...	The best thing that ever happened to me in school was...

CHAPTER 4

Homework According to Hoyle

Helping Your Child Become Organized for the Long-Term

I n my job, I work with underachieving college students. The ones that I see who are flunking out or doing very poorly have zero organizational skills. Most of them never held a job so that they did not have to make independent decisions, take responsibility for tasks, and receive positive and negative feedback. They had tutors and too much parental help, and still obtained high grade point averages throughout their elementary and secondary education. This is an example of getting good grades but flunking Life 101. If you want your child to truly succeed, at some point he or she will have to be able to fly solo. Here are some ideas to help you both get to that point.

Practice Paying Attention Amidst Distraction

Sit your child in front of a TV program with a pad and paper. Read him some assignments and ask him to write them down. Then read a similar assignment and ask him to write it down without any distraction. Check the accuracy of both. Or you can have one family member read from a book or magazine aloud while the child is attempting to write down the assignment. This technique effectively mimics what goes on in some classrooms when the teacher gives the assignment to be written down.

If your child has problems copying from the board, write some assignments on a big piece of paper or dry erase board, then having the child practice copying them down with some distraction present. In addition to teaching your child to filter out distractions more easily, this can also be a way to prove to your child or teenager that she could get done sooner if she studied in peace and quiet. If, for example, your child wants to do homework with noise (like music), and you think that the child needs less stimulation, time how long it takes the child to complete an assignment with the noise, and to complete a similar assignment with no noise.

Help Your Child Build Independence

Once in a while I have taken a Homework Sabbatical, enjoying a hiatus from homework coaching so that I can meet other obligations in life, or because I am burnt out with homework supervision. Though the grades may go down a bit, your child or teenager is able to experience some independence that can be developmentally advantageous. This teaches them to create their own strategies for self-regulation and organization. Kids can develop independence by doing chores, cleaning up after themselves, and cooking. For teenagers, getting part-time employment like baby-sitting or mowing lawns can foster independence.

Teach Your Child to Talk Through Problems and to Self-Reinforce

Do you ever talk to yourself? It helps a lot of us to stay focused and organized. Teach your child to ask about an assignment, "What am I supposed to do?" "What should I do first?" "Now what?" As your child begins to have an internal dialogue, also teach positive self-reinforcement. Students need to mentally "pat themselves on the back" for a job well done. It helps to keep them motivated. Teach them to say to themselves, "Good job," "I got it done," "Whew, that was hard, but I did it."

Permit Your Student to Create Organizational Strategies

Encourage your child to develop his or her own organizational skills. My son started writing reminders on his arm. At first the practice—letters scrawled on his entire forearm—seemed ridiculous, but he doesn't do it often, and it helps him to remember. He used to leave his clarinet in front of the door so he would have to trip on it leaving his room. Lately, I see him leaving himself notes in the bathroom (if your child does this, be sure not to throw these out when you clean the bathroom!) and the floor of his room. I let his organizational systems alone, since he has to be organized when he is an adult.

Homework Diagnostic # 3, (see p. 54) which the student should complete alone, offers strategies to help the student ten years old and older learn to approach homework problems independently. You may want to make copies for your student so that he or she can use a fresh one when confronted with a new homework hurdle.

Teach Your Child How to Know When to Ask for Help

Under what circumstances do you expect your child to ask a teacher or parent for help? Many kids don't know or are too proud to ask. Make sure your child realizes that everyone needs help from time to time. Here are a few ideas of when outside help might be necessary:

- The task is hard and it would take a lot less time if the student got help;

- The student is overwhelmed, having a homework meltdown, or sick;

- The student has no idea what to do;

- The student has exhausted all the ways that they know how to complete the task.

This applies to parents and students alike. The next chapter will address ways to get help outside the home.

HOMEWORK DIAGNOSTIC # 3: Homework Strategies Checklist for Students

Study Environment

❏ Organize study space differently.

❏ Decrease noise in study space. Put on a fan or music to drown out distractions, or move to a quieter place.

❏ Make a distraction screen using a tri-fold board or cardboard box.

❏ Study with a friend.

Organizational Ideas

❏ Make copies of papers that are important, if you might lose them.

❏ Color code subjects so that notebook matches color or book, for example.

❏ Put papers, hole-punched, in binder.

❏ Make a homework box with notebook paper, pens, pencils, markers, etc.

❏ Clean out notebook/backpack/binder more often.

Study Strategies

❏ Figure out what order to do assignments at home (easiest to hardest?).

❏ Agree on the number and length of time for breaks with your homework coach.

❏ Make a list of fun ways to spend your short breaks. Use the kitchen timer or a clock.

❏ Read difficult material out loud.

❏ Call someone in your class if you have a question or forgot your book.

❏ If you need help from your homework coach, and she/he works, save that subject for after the homework coach is home.

❏ Find a tutor or tutoring program.

Time Management

❏ Cut down on extracurricular activities, if necessary.

❏ Use homework websites to save time.

❏ Make a to-do list.

❏ Use your planner wisely.

HOMEWORK DIAGNOSTIC # 3: Homework Strategies Checklist for Students (cont.)

Writing/Spelling

❏ Use a proofreading checklist. Most teachers distribute a proofreading checklist containing common grammar tips, like checking for correct punctuation and capitalization. Ask your teacher if you don't have one.

❏ Use the writing tips on http://www.factmonster.com/homework/writingskills1.html .

❏ Read written material out loud to see if it makes sense.

❏ Use Scrabble tiles for spelling words.

Reading

❏ Use books on tape or CD.

❏ Use Post-it notes to mark important parts so that it is easier to answer questions when you are done.

❏ Read it out loud to help yourself pay attention.

Projects/Reports

❏ Make note of references as you go along and in the proper format so that when you get to the end, it's done.

❏ Work ahead on projects.

❏ Oral reports: practice in front of mirror or for family members several times.

Test Preparation

❏ Make flashcards.

❏ Use memorization strategies like rhyme, linking information to something you like, making concepts into a picture, putting it to music, pretending to give a lecture or class

❏ Figure out how often the teacher gives tests or quizzes for each class.

❏ Make an audiotape of material to learn and listen to it a few times.

❏ Make a test for yourself including true-false, multiple choice, matching, fill-in-the-blank, or definitions.

Feelings About Homework

❏ Speak in a calm manner to your homework coach, even when frustrated.

❏ Limit the amount of complaining/venting to the homework coach.

❏ Videotape favorite show to watch after homework, if allowed.

❏ Increase positive self-talk like, "I'll get this done."

❏ Remind yourself that you can't work as fast as some kids but it doesn't mean that you are stupid.

❏ Headaches, stomachaches, and other aches and pains can be related to stress. If you are getting a lot of these, improve your stress management by talking to someone about your stress, listening to music, or getting some exercise.

CHAPTER 5

Low-Tech and High-Tech Homework Aids

Whether you are still the full-time homework coach or your student is learning to become more of an independent, organized worker, you'll find that very few problems can't be solved or at least helped with a gadget or two. Although these aids are not for everyone or every problem, it's good to be aware of them and how they can help. They can be incorporated into your Homework Plan at any stage.

Low-Tech Solutions

- **Dry erase board:** Dry erase boards can be useful for helping your child with homework, for your child to use instead of scratch paper, for studying, and for leaving reminder notes for yourself. We have a dry erase board on the fridge for family communication and there is one in the bathroom for my sons use for notes like "remember gym clothes." You can get a dry erase board that will hang on a doorknob, and all kinds of other portable boards. This is the technology aid that we have used the most at our house, along with office supplies.

- **Office supplies:** All kinds of office supplies exist to help disorganized people: spiral-bound sets of plastic pocket folders, brightly colored plastic portfolios of various sizes, and folders in all sorts of colors and sizes. Whether your child has a report to do on germs or George Washington, never underestimate the attractiveness of say, a bright red folder or envelope as he or she goes about a difficult task. For some children, office supplies give an element of control and predictability to an out-of-control, unpredictable situation. Many students find it helps to color code their materials for each subject, coordinating book color with notebook color. Mead has developed color-coded organizational materials for four subjects: math, language arts, science, and social studies.

  Office supplies can also be a way to reinforce your child for working hard: an orange gel pen, a fancy mechanical pencil, or similar merchandise can serve as incentives. With the popularity of dollar and discount stores, these purchases need not be expensive.

- **Post-it notes or flags:** You can use these self-adhesive, removable notes to mark definitions or important points in a book so to avoid the flipping back and looking for it. They can also be used to leave reminders in notebooks, books, and to help organize materials. For a few dollars, you can find a pen or highlighter with the pop-up flags built into it.

- **Tri-fold or presentation board:** You can get these foldable, cardboard, three-part boards at any office supply store or reuse one your student had for a project. Use it at the kitchen table to create a less distracting study space for your child. It is a portable way to provide your child with study space. You can get creative and attach things to the board like study tips, a place for pencils, and so on.

High-Tech Solutions

- **Copy machine:** Having a copy machine at home can save time in making flashcards and is very useful for children or teenagers who lose papers. This way, they can make extra copies of important material in case they lose it. Some simple copy machines are about $100. Computer scanners or digital cameras can also be used for this purpose, and many inexpensive multipurpose printer/scanner/copiers are now available for home use.

- **Cell phone with calendar feature:** If you can afford it and want your child to have a cell phone, some of them have organizational programs, like computerized schedule organizers, built into them. Kids like electronic devices and they love their cell phones. Even very disorganized teenagers have their cell phones wherever they go. They are more likely to use something that they carry all the time.

- **Voice recorder pen or microcassette recorder:** Some teachers tend to give the assignment or change the assignment when the kids are about to leave, making it hard for a child who copies or writes slowly to get it down right. Voice recorder pens and microcassette recorders are good for kids in this situation. They can also help those who do better with auditory input and need reminders, like "remember gym clothes." They vary in price as well as the length of the recording time. Check with the school about the policy on tape recording; one student needed to make the reminder recording outside of the classroom.

- **Online dictionaries:** If it is a terrible chore for your child to find things in the dictionary, try online dictionaries such as www.m-w.com and www.dictionary.com. They can be a big time-saver and morale booster, especially if you put the dictionary on your Favorites list (if you do not know what a Favorites list is, ask your young person) so your child can get into it quickly. Although it is important for children to learn proper dictionary skills, the child with executive function problems will spend hours on something that could take 20 or 30 minutes.

- **Electronic spell checker:** Tools like the Franklin Spelling Ace can be useful in the early primary grades if your child has trouble with spelling, although you will need to check with your child's school about the feasibility of using it in the classroom. If the child is really off on the spelling, however, this device is of little help. Consider making a "word wall": Buy a roll of cash register paper tape, write the misspelled words on the paper, and tape them to the wall in the child's room.

- **Calculator:** Students need different calculators depending on the level of math class they are taking, especially in middle school and high school. For most elementary schools, an inexpensive calculator without a lot of bells and whistles should be fine. For a disorganized child, a calculator with more buttons than needed complicates the task and can be distracting.

- **Tape player with variable speed controls:** For young people with reading disabilities who need to use audiobooks, sometimes the speed at which books on tape are presented can be too fast. Some tape recorders have a variable speed feature allowing your child to slow down the tape. Some school systems or libraries will loan you one of these if your child has documented need.

- **Franklin KID240 Speaking Homework Wiz:** This device has a sort of fancy talking dictionary and games with words. Like a spell-checker, you can enter a word to see if it is spelled correctly, and it also has a feature to teach penmanship. It costs about $50.00.

- **Personal Digital Assistant (PDA):** Handheld devices are particularly popular for high school and college students. It makes sense, however, that children must first be able to use a planner on paper before switching to the PDA, unless they are being taught by the teacher to use electronic support devices.

- **Computer and Internet access:** Although the computer is a standard in many homes, not all families can afford them, or Internet connectivity. If you do not have a computer or yours is broken, some schools lend them, most public libraries have computers available for student use, and some businesses, such as Kinkos, rent computer time. If you need help with how to pick a computer, *How to Help Your Child With Homework* (Radencich & Shumm, 1996) has a great chapter on this (pp. 122-131).

CHAPTER 6

Your Homework Allies

The Teacher, the School, and Other Supports

P arents often feel like they have to do it all themselves. This only leads to burnout and frustration, to the detriment of their own sanity and their relationships with their children. After all, if there is a plumbing problem, and you don't have plumbing expertise, you call a plumber. Why do we think we can solve homework problems alone? Your child's school and your community most likely offer a wealth of expertise and assistance to kids and parents in the homework trenches.

Tips for Working with the Teacher and the School

No matter what other resources you seek in your homework journey, it's always worth it to work as closely as possible with your child's teacher and other school personnel.

The Teacher

Many teachers will go above and beyond the call of duty—or their teaching contracts—to help a student who has difficulty. Both my sons have had hardworking teachers who leave the school building long after the other teachers have gone home—calm, patient teachers with great ideas, like Miss Farmer of Lomond Elementary School in Shaker Heights, Ohio, who suggested that we make a "word wall" in second grade (see p. 60). Nevertheless, not every teacher will "get" your child, and some teachers will dislike him or her. The teacher may tell you that your child is lazy, not paying attention, or imply that you are trying to get a not-so-bright kid to meet your expectations of brilliance.

Regardless of whether you have a good impression of the teacher, or whether your child likes the teacher, develop a working relationship with him or her. You are stuck with this teacher for the remainder of the school year.

Think "business meeting" when you are talking to you child's teacher. For example, one teacher chastised students who did not immediately come up with the answer to a question by saying, "duh," a colloquialism that is the slang equivalent of saying "You stupid idiot." This alienated the student (who had slow information processing) and infuriated the parent. Here is an example of how the parent might approach this teacher the *wrong* way:

"He told me that you have been saying 'duh' when he does not answer a question right away. What were you thinking?! He has had trouble in school for years, and I am already taking him to a therapist because he thinks he is stupid. I don't need you to make his self-esteem any worse than it already is!"

A better way to discuss this problem would be for the parent to say, "I don't know if you are aware that it can take my son a few minutes to answer a question because he has unusually slow cognitive processing speed. He says that you are saying, 'duh' when he cannot answer immediately. I think this makes him feel bad. What might work is to ask the question, call on him, and if he doesn't have an answer immediately, then say, 'I will come back to you in a minute for your answer.'"

The problem with the first option is that you are criticizing the teacher and accusing her of being mean without knowing her perspective. Perhaps the teacher thinks it is funny to say 'duh,' although for the life of me I cannot imagine a teacher being that insensitive. Maybe it only happened a few times and then she realized it wasn't funny. The second alternative is calmer, nonaccusatory, and suggests a solution to the problem without being pushy. It also gives the teacher a chance to save face if she made a mistake and didn't think about what she was doing. A general rule of thumb is to think carefully about what you want to say and what you would like to get out of the conversation before you talk with the teacher. Never, never get into arguing or shouting with a teacher, and avoid going to the principal to "tell" on the teacher unless the teacher does not respond to calls or requests for a conference.

Attend the school's open house and try to get to know your child's teacher. Offer to help out if he sends around a sign-up sheet for classroom help or support. Do not try to discuss your individual child at open house. This is a time for teachers to tell you how they run their classroom and what they expect from students. Consider open house a piece of homework detective work: when is the spelling test, every Friday? Are the science labs every week or every two weeks?

Don't miss the parent-teacher conference. Many teachers offer a variety of times to accommodate working and nonworking parents. Don't be afraid to ask for an alternative time if they do not offer one. During the conference, let the teacher know how long you are working on the homework. It helps teachers to know the range of time assignments take students. Teachers may also be willing to make accommodations for some students. For example, maybe the student could do 10 math problems instead of 20, or perhaps the teacher would allow the parent to write out the spelling sentences that the student has created. Use the conference to learn about problems your child is having, as well as strengths. Bring some questions and take notes. Ask the teacher if he has suggestions, and don't get defensive about the feedback. I don't always agree with what the teachers say, but I think about the information and blow off steam later with a friend or family member if it makes me angry. Remember, this is a business meeting.

The Guidance Counselor

Guidance counselors vary tremendously in levels of knowledge and expertise. Some are what I call "nicey-nicey" people who like children but have few problem-solving or psychoeducational skills. A good guidance counselor is the person your child can check in with, who you can check in with, and who serves as a liaison between you and the teaching team. If you are very, very lucky, you will get someone like Ms. Judy Braden of Marshall Middle School in McCandless, PA, who possesses an extraordinary amount of knowledge about the learning and emotional challenges children face in middle school. Get to know your child's guidance counselor regardless of your personal opinion of their skills. Remember that the guidance counselor is responsible for a large number of students, and consequently their parents. Avoid long, rambling calls or e-mails. Before you call, collect your thoughts, make a list of your concerns, make your point and listen politely for suggestions.

Wish Lists

I have two wish lists of policies that I always hope teachers and administrators will consider implementing. Any of these items would be a boon to a student with homework difficulties and his or her parents. Consider advocating for these ideas, whether directly or through the school's parent-teacher organization.

For Teachers

- Ask students how long your homework assignments take, and modify if needed.

- Teach organizational and time management skills if you do not already.

- If a student is sick (and has a doctor's or parent's note), don't expect the child to make up every single assignment.

- If a student misses assignments due to illness, record grades as "incomplete," not as a failing grade. Recording a failing grade adds insult to injury.

- Make student's grades private, including reading levels. All student test scores should be private.

- Put assignments online, or on the homework hotline, weekly.

- Give all the homework assignments at the start of the week.

- Provide choices and creative options on homework assignments, such as "Complete a written report, make a video, or write a skit on the assigned topic."

- Use peer tutoring carefully so the bright students don't do all the work.

- Offer "homework passes" (one "skip-the-homework-night" per grading period)

- Promote or develop after school homework programs with administrators, and in-school programs for organizationally challenged children.

- Make flashcards in class.

- Put as much information online as you can. This benefits you by eliminating excuses in households where students have easy computer access.

- Acknowledge students' feelings about homework.

- Don't assume that underachievers are lazy. It is a red flag that something else is wrong.

- Give parents homework tips.

For School Administrators

- Develop programs for organizationally challenged students.

- Increase the amount of time teachers use in class to teach students to make and use flashcards.

- Ensure that your teachers use the homework hotline or website if your school has one. Check that it is being used and respond to parent complaints in this regard.

- Consider training or hiring an ADHD specialist for your school district; psychologists are valuable consultants on this topic.

- Budget money for homework clubs.

Other School-Based Supports

The school may offer a variety of other programs and services that can make a difference to both you and your child in the homework struggle. If you see a program listed here that your school does not offer, consider working with the parent-teacher organization to advocate for and implement a similar idea.

Study Hall Tutoring

In some schools, tutors are available during study halls for one-to-one help during regularly scheduled free periods. Students tell me that this is very helpful, but it is not available at all schools. If this is not available at your school, you could ask whether the teacher in charge of the study hall is willing to answer questions. For some schools, there is a tutoring room where students can come during free periods or after school for tutoring. If your child is likely to need a lot of extra in-school help, make sure that his or her schedule allows for a study hall.

After-School Programs

Some after-school programs, used by two-parent families where both parents work, or by single parents who work, have excellent resources for supporting homework completion. In cities with federal, state, and local funding for after-school programs, research shows that such so-called "2 to 6" programs with homework help and tutoring enhance learning (www.educationworld.com). Programs are often school-based, but not every school has one, and availability may be limited if it does. If a school-based program is unavailable, many religious institutions, nonprofit groups, and community centers also have after-school programs. Check with other parents before enrolling your child if you can, as many are more recreational and do not focus on homework. When my kids were small, I had them in an after-school program where homework was supposed to get done but never was completed.

Homework Clubs

In eighth grade, my son attended a twice-weekly Homework Club run by one of the teachers, Mr. Dotillo of Marshall Middle School, in Wexford, PA, for students who needed support in getting the homework done. As opposed to the social and recreational focus of many after-school programs, this was a homework-focused and primarily homework-driven environment. The afternoon started out with a candy bar and a soft drink, and then everyone settled down to do homework. I loved the homework club for several reasons. First, my son really enjoyed it! At first, I think he looked forward to the snack, but he quickly developed a relationship with the teacher, who supported him to work independently. He looked forward to Homework Club, hated to miss it if he was sick, and he came home with almost all of the homework done after a couple hours. And it felt like a vacation for me as the homework coach. I didn't need to call, e-mail, or have conferences with the teacher—it gave me a much-needed break.

I do not know how many schools have Homework Clubs, or what the structure of such clubs might be. It strikes me that it is a low-cost program that would meet a need in many school districts, however. It seems that the combination of an adult who is not the parent, and peers in the same situation creates a supportive environment in which to get the work done. If your school does not have one, it might be a good idea for the parent-teacher organization to advocate for such a program. The downside is that Homework Club may be scheduled at a time when kids have to choose between other extracurricular activities and the club. Having it available every day so that students could come when they are not scheduled for other activities would be beneficial. Homework clubs can also occur in the context of the child's religious affiliation (i.e. Homework Clubs at churches or synagogues).

School Programs for Organizationally Challenged Students

Some school districts are starting to offer variations on the traditional curriculum that may help disorganized students. For example, North Allegheny Intermediate High School in Wexford, PA, offers a program emphasizing organization and study skills for a limited number of students. It is not a special education program, though special education students may be in it, nor is it a program for troublemakers or particularly for underachievers. Enrolled students have the regular 9th and 10th grade curriculum with more organizational support and teaching. Homework organization and methods of successfully completing assignments are incorporated into the curricula. For example, students in the program receive "Need to Know" lists (study guides), make flashcards, develop test-taking skills, and maintain an organized binder. Teachers, counselors, or parents may refer a student to the program, or students may self-refer. For this program, most students are referred in 9th grade and stay until 10th grade; a smaller number enter in 10th grade or are ready to leave the program after one year.

Also, Pittsburgh Public Schools has a charter school in which a student is given a computer with preinstalled software to use at home for completing the high school curriculum online. The student has an online homeroom teacher, and teachers for different classes. Students can work at will. This is great for home-schooled and other nontraditional students.

The rules that apply to a regular high school appear to apply to such charter schools. For example, if a student cannot complete high school in four years for a good reason, they can remain in the program. I have seen these types of programs as most helpful for a teenager with behavioral or emotional problems that make adjustment to a typical high school environment impossible. An online high school can also be advantageous for a student with a chronic medical condition or one that needs to work to help support the family. The only trouble with these for a student with chronic homework problems is this educational environment requires that the students be able to keep themselves on task, so you need to carefully consider whether this is right for your teen.

Online Textbooks

Prentice Hall and Discovery School have partnered to put textbooks online. http://phschool.com/successnet. Other companies may be doing this as well. Advocate for online texts for your school if you would like to see students lugging less in their backpacks. This is a handy solution for students who forget books.

Homework Online or Homework Hotline

Increasingly, teachers have websites or phone hotlines that contain the homework for the week. If your school does not have either of these, start working with your parent-teacher organization to get one set up. If homework is online, it encourages teachers to develop a homework plan for the entire week. This approach can help the disorganized student a lot, because he can break tasks up into doable parts based on difficulty of the task. If you have a computer and Internet access, it is also a great idea to ask teachers to e-mail you the homework for the week. If you do not have a computer, see if you can work out another plan with the teacher or guidance counselor to get your child's assignments on a weekly basis.

Supports Outside the School

Not all schools have the programs and services described in the last section. And depending on the teachers' contracts, the hours they work, their personal commitments, or other jobs, they may not be available to help a struggling student at a time that is convenient to the student and the parent, or at all. Finally, sometimes the type of help your child needs is truly beyond what the teacher or the school can offer, in school or after hours. In these situations, you may need to seek help from other sources.

Tutors

If for whatever reason, the school cannot do what you hope they would do, and you have made reasonable attempts to get extra time and it isn't forthcoming, then consider a tutor. If your community has a local tutoring program, or if you can afford a private tutor, this can be a great help. What advantages has a tutor got over you? Tutors who are trained in education will know some study strategies and shortcuts that you may not know. If you are the homework coach, you have probably experienced periods when your son or daughter is tired of answering to you and you are tired of monitoring homework. The tutor is a neutral person to whom your child is likely to listen. It leaves the parent time to deal with other tasks, like making supper without responding to questions about schoolwork, thus lowering everyone's stress levels.

Tutors come in various shapes and sizes. Some professional tutoring outfits tend to hire teachers who want a second job or want to work part-time. Individual freelance tutors may be retired teachers, college students, bright high school students, or folks who want to work part-time. Check the tutor's credentials and approach to the subject matter and find out what you are getting for your money. You want a tutor who will work with your existing homework plan. It is nice if the tutor can come to your home, but this may not always be possible. If the tutor wants to meet in a public place, such as the library, be sensitive to your child's need not to have everyone in town know that he or she needs tutoring.

If you can't afford to pay a tutor, could you trade or barter tutoring time with another parent or family member who has expertise in the area where your child needs help? For example, could you provide tutoring or enrichment for your niece or your neighbor's son (say, musical ability or a foreign language) in exchange for having Uncle Phil the physicist or your neighbor Emma the engineer help your son with math? Or is there an older brother or sister who could serve as a tutor? Sometimes religious institutions have tutoring programs that are available at low or no cost. You could also start a co-op tutoring program of your own by working with other parents. Finally, maybe you could get a high school student to volunteer as a tutor. After all, volunteer work looks good on college applications, and many high schools now require a certain amount of community service to graduate.

Counseling

If you are in a homework rut, you may need to see a psychologist, social worker, or counselor. Parents tell me that they come to a therapist when they are out of ideas, the student is not doing well academically, the student feels badly about him/herself, the student is getting in trouble at home or at school, or it has been a bad school year. Also consider professional help if you or your child are experiencing depression, burnout, or an inability to control your anger. Therapists can help both you and your child with stress management, anger management, depression, self-esteem, and so on.

You can get names of licensed psychologists and other mental health professionals from your insurance company or your pediatrician. If you cannot get names of therapists this way, you can try your State or Local Psychological Association (e.g. Pennsylvania Psychological Association or Pittsburgh Psychological Association), or the American Psychological Association (www.APA.org).

During the summer in my private practice, I see many kids who had a bad school year. I advise some children and teenagers (and their parents) to take the summer off from developing strategies to manage their organizational problems. I want their parents to have a break too. You don't have to be a psychologist to figure out that the rat race is not good for families.

CHAPTER 7

Coaches' Corner

Tips and Techniques to Help Parents Keep it Together

Everyday Techniques

Turn It Off

The school bus is coming, or you are heading home from work. Turn off your cell phone, TV, radio, CD player, DVD player, or pager. Stop checking your e-mail and talking on the phone. Get in the proper frame of mind to manage homework theatre. A soccer coach gets her equipment together—soccer balls, first aid kit, water jug—and you must gather your equipment too. For me, it is a pot of after-school coffee, my glasses, scrap paper, and something to read if I need to be on standby to check on work. I cook during homework coaching, but if you are organizationally challenged, this is not a good idea at first. Try telling your kids, "I'll look it over after I get this in the oven."

Keep Your Cool

We all know that we shouldn't be yelling, that a calm, reassuring voice is our best ally in the homework battle. But we are all human, and some of us yell. Here is my favorite anger management example:

You get in a minor car accident. Another driver runs a stop sign while talking on a cell phone, hitting your vehicle. You may be tempted to scream, "You bleep-bleep idiot! You just ran the stop sign because you are too stupid to STOP TALKING AND WATCH THE ROAD…" Now the cell phone driver is unlikely to respond, "Oh, my, are you all right? Yes, that was dumb of me. I am *so* sorry. Let me just write you a check right now so you won't be inconvenienced by having to call your insurance company. And I feel so terrible that I have caused you any trouble." What is likely to transpire is a shouting match, which will not help anything. Even in major league baseball, you can't get your way by shouting at the umpire. They kick you out of the game if you say bad words.

The major problem that I see in parents with respect to stress management is that they do not decompress before talking to the child, or they don't allow the child to decompress before the child talks to them. We have to teach our children to calm themselves down, but we have to calm down too. So when the bad words start, or the bad attitude, the first step for you and your child is to calm down. If you are disorganized yourself and your child is taxing your already meager organizational skills, you may be a bit short-tempered. Can you get a difficult task accomplished right after someone yells at you? No. And neither can your child. Avoid name-calling. I have worked with parents who call their children things like "stupid," "moron," and "idiot." Your child is unlikely to be motivated by these words.

If your child is having a homework problem, you need to practice good stress management. You know the drill: get exercise, eat healthy, get a good night's sleep. And yes, take it easy on the alcohol and caffeine. If you need to blow off steam, try keeping a journal. Or talk to a friend out of earshot of the child. Give yourself a pep talk before homework time. And if none of this works, maybe you need to seek therapy for anger management.

Divide Your Attention Wisely

We all try to divide our time equally among our children, but when you have a child doing poorly in school, this gets skewed. Be honest with the child or children getting less time without putting down the other child. Most parents know that it is not a good idea to compare your children's academic skills. Make appointments with each child for homework help or to check in about other concerns. Say things like, "Joan, I need to help Ellen with her math, but later I will check in with you to see what sorts of assignments you are working on."

There are special considerations for the larger family, though there is little research on this topic. If you are struggling with the homework demands imposed by two or three children, can you imagine the homework of eight to ten children? When many children have homework to complete daily, positive modeling can occur (or negative role modeling, if older siblings do not do their homework). One thing that happens is the older children help the younger children. Even in my small household of two children, my older son has become a patient teacher after years of giving his brother help with advanced math. The two of them could be arguing all day, but if the older son needs to answer questions about German grammar, they switch into neutral homework mode. I think that both of them have learned to accept positive and negative feedback. (Feedback means you listen to what someone says and think about it, even if you disagree. It is something that many adults need to learn too.)

Though this is a good system, it is still important for parents to have a clear idea about strengths and weaknesses of each child. If you have a large number of children, it is especially important to have some kind of organization at home.

Work with the Other Parent

Parents can learn to work together in creative ways. One day after I officiated at a homework meltdown, I had to get to the office since

I see clients after school and in the evening. After reestablishing some level of calmness after my son's rough day, I called his dad and left a voice mail at work apprising him of the homework situation. I also left a few suggestions about coping with the homework crisis. This strategy gives advance notice and planning time for the other homework coach (i.e. "I may not have time to work out tonight"). It also means that the other parent can go to work, meeting or social function without worrying about what is going on in the homework trenches. Even if you are divorced from the child's other parent, you can both still be homework coaches—more in this in the last section of this chapter.

The Morning Shuffle

Generally, you want to avoid doing homework in the morning; it can set a bad tone for the day for both parent and child. Doing homework early in the morning also increases levels of anxiety and that we are trying to avoid. Sometimes you get to a point in the evening homework where you have to stop, however. After all, parents have stressors in their lives relating to work, care of elderly, life crises, health problems and so on. It is okay to save something like a spelling word review for the morning. Make sure it is something that you can do while you complete your own morning routine. I have spent many a morning applying cosmetics while quizzing my son on second-grade spelling words or eighth-grade science vocabulary.

Discourage Cheating

Okay, we all know that cheating is bad, right? But late at night, who among us has not said at least once, "Write this down"—effectively doing the assignment for the student. You would be surprised how many parents actually do their child's homework and do not consider this to be cheating. But if you make a habit of this, you deprive your child of the opportunity to feel good about him or herself, even though it may seem to provide a temporary solution to the problem. Do not do your child's homework.

Then there is the kind of cheating where the student copies from another student. If you catch your child copying from a friend, or the teacher tells you he caught the child copying, take it seriously and discourage this practice. Also, plagiarism has become considerably easier due to the Internet. Checking on cheating has also become easier on the Internet, however. Teach your child about plagiarism. Some children are not aware that you cannot copy exactly from other's words.

Cheating sometimes occurs out of desperation when the student is overwhelmed and sees no other way out. If you get a better handle on homework drama, you will rarely, if ever have to worry about this problem. Most kids feel good about themselves when they do their own work.

Find the Humor

When all else fails, it is important to have a sense of humor about homework. Laughter is a great stress-buster. One book that I love, called *No More Homework, No More Tests! Kids' Favorite Funny School Poems,* by Bruce Lansky, is filled with silly poems that are sure to make children under the age of 12 giggle. Many nationally syndicated comic strips employ themes of school and homework trouble. You can download jokes from the Internet on homework, and numerous homework t-shirts that may amuse your student are available (one of my clients recently came to therapy wearing a t-shirt that said, "Flying monkeys took my homework."). On the Internet, there is a website where parents can obtain—for a fee— a Bachelor's, Master's or PhD of Homework Assistance. Whatever you do, try to lighten up and you will feel a lot less like a Homework Bully.

Tips for Disorganized Parents

Often, as I talk with families about providing structure and systems of doing homework a different way, the parent tells me, "I am really disorganized myself. How can I help my child if I can't keep myself organized?" or "I think that I have adult ADHD, what should I do?" If you have a significant attention problem, or you think you do, consult your primary care physician or get an evaluation with a mental health professional. Here are some basic techniques that may help you, however. You can find many more resources on the Internet and at the library.

Break it Down

I found an article about how to organize the home and office at http://www.help4adhd.org/living/organdtime/organization. This article recommends that you break all tasks down into smaller steps. So, for example, while your child is organizing for the afternoon, whether you're home or checking in by phone, plan your own approach to the evening. See the Sample Schedules for ideas on organizing your and your child's tasks.

Make Lists

One key to organization is making lists. As I recommended for students, try making several lists—to do today, to do this week, and long-term goals. If you are not so good at making lists, there is a website (www.lists.com) that can help you out. Figure out the best place to maintain your lists: in a planner or organizer, a Personal Digital Assistant (PDA), on a dry erase or bulletin board. Lists are only as good as your ability to *do* the items on the list, so pay attention that you are not expecting too much of yourself. I like to physically cross things off the list because it gives me a sense of completion and helps me not to get overwhelmed by the remaining things on the list.

Sample Schedules

Weekday:

4:00 P.M.–5:00 P.M.	Help with social studies map project. Do load of laundry. Check my e-mail. Make a few phone calls for work.
5:00 P.M.–5:30 P.M.	Child takes a break so I can start supper, or child does an assignment with which she is unlikely to need help.
5:30 P.M.–6:00 P.M.	Check homework while dinner cooks.
6:00 P.M.–7:00 P.M.	Eat, clean up, relax.
7:00 P.M.	Remaining homework.

Weekend:

7:00 A.M.–10:00 A.M.	Cartoons, leisure, downtime
10:00 A.M.–Noon	Take kids to sports, arts or religious class. Do errands that are on the way or close to those locations.
Noon–12:30 P.M.	Lunch
1:00 P.M.–2:00 P.M.	Child does one hour of homework or reading. Parent makes list of other errands and most efficient way to get them done. Parent might also be doing household chores that allow availability to the student.
2:00 P.M.–4:00 P.M.	Errands, play dates, shopping.
4:00 P.M.–4:30 P.M.	Another half hour of homework if necessary.
5:00 P.M.–Lights Out	Break time!!!

Take a Good, Hard Look at your Schedule

Many families these days are overscheduled. This results in running around every weekday and every weekend. Children with attention and organization problems *need time at home* to get the homework done and they may need *more* time than other students. I have seen many families where children are trying to do homework in the car in between school and sports. If you had an important project to do for work or home, could you do your best in the car? Yet, when I give input that I think the family has too much on the schedule, parents do not really want to hear it. My opinion as a developmental psychologist is that children need downtime in order to manage stress and to provide opportunities for unstructured recreation. Parents usually benefit from this kind of time too.

Also, a parent who is organizationally challenged, who might even have an undiagnosed attention deficit disorder, will become *more* disorganized as the various commitments (and the running around to meet them) increase. When parents run around a lot, they become overwhelmed even under the best of circumstances. Most people's organizational strategies break down as their stress level goes up.

Hire an Organizing Service

There are many small companies devoted to helping you organize your household or office. Most major cities have professional associations of home organizers. If you can afford this, it could be well worth the money to get some help for *your* organizational systems. After all, how can you expect your child to manage his or her organizational troubles if you set a terrible example. If you can't afford a professional, ask a family member or friend who is more organized than you are to assist you in this task. Or, spend a vacation day or two with the goal of all the family members working to organize the household.

Reward Yourself

As I mentioned earlier, being a good parent is hard work at times, especially if you have one or more underachieving youngsters. Figure out what you need to do to reward yourself when you maintain some level of organization. After a tough homework night, do something to reward yourself as well.

Techniques for Parents with Special Challenges

Now that we have covered ideas for the organizationally challenged parent, I'd like to offer some strategies for parents in atypical circumstances.

Homework In Two Homes

This can be a recipe for disaster. Because split custody is popular, a child is with a different parent part of the week. It is best if both parents participate in homework coaching (Okay, I know some of you are laughing), but the reality is that one parent usually handles most of the homework. If only one parent participates in homework coaching, be clear with the child or teenager that they are accountable to *that parent* when it comes to homework. The child might ask questions of the other parent or stepparent, but the primary homework coaching will fall on one person. People who are divorced parents know that things are not always even or fair. Or if Mom is the one who is good at math and the child is at Dad's, there needs to be flexibility to work this out. This is very hard to pull off unless the parents have a cooperative parenting relationship. There are many good books out there on co-parenting, like *The Co-Parenting Survival Guide* (Zimmerman 2001).

In some cases, parents may still be engaged in an ongoing battle, shouting at one another by phone, making disparaging remarks about one another in front of the kids, or not even on speaking terms with one another. This creates an organizational nightmare. Keep in mind that the less stress there is in the family, the more likely that homework will get done. Kids are almost always adversely affected when parents persist in frequent court initiatives that, although important to them, keep levels of conflict high.

Also, try to work it out without putting school personnel in the middle of the conflicts. If the homework battle somehow merges with the divorce issues, you probably need to seek professional help. In my practice, I see a hefty number of kids whose parents are locked into conflict in a way that affects their ability to raise the children. A good psychologist, social worker, or counselor with training in family therapy and parent guidance can help with this problem.

Single Parents

Many aspects of single parenting can be difficult, but with respect to homework, the most frequent problems for single parents tend to be no break from the homework stress, job constraints, higher levels of stress than two-parent families, and a household budget that may rule out tutoring as an option. Parents who lack a partner to give them a break from homework heartache should identify one or two family members or friends who can help out from time to time. Homework clubs, after-school programs where homework help is provided, or community-based tutoring programs can also provide respite for the overwhelmed single parent.

Parents with Chronic Illness

Parents in treatment for cancer, heart disease, or any number of other medical problems can lack the energy to cope with common parenting problems like homework. A parent who is undergoing chemotherapy, for example, may be in no condition to help a son or daughter who is flunking math, or to figure out what to do about a child who won't bring home assignments.

If a child who has a parent with significant illness is having homework troubles, the first thing to do is to tap your family's existing support network of relatives, friends, or clergy. Sometimes a teacher will take a special interest in mentoring the child during parent illness. Mr. Chris Panos of Marshall Middle School is one such teacher; his emotional support of student during parental ill-ness extended long after the student moved on to the next grade. If necessary, consult a professional, like a psychologist or social worker, because a child's feelings about the parent's illness can affect his or her homework performance, even if he or she hasn't historically has homework problems. It is important for the school to be aware of a parent's chronic illness, though the parent's diagnosis or medi-cal condition need not be shared with the school. You would be sur-prised to know the number of teachers who quietly go about pro-viding emotional support or tolerating late assignments for stu-dents with a health crisis in the family.

Child with Chronic Illness

My son has asthma and has missed at minimum 10 days of school per year. The year he had mononucleosis, we hit an all-time high of three months out of school. This level of illness is a homework train wreck. Try to act as early as is reasonable to keep your child from falling too far behind. If the child is hospitalized frequently, there are in-hospital schools. If the child is cared for at home, you can request in-home teaching, although in my experience, it can take a little while to get this implemented.

You need to have very good communication with the school if your child is sick often or has a chronic medical condition. Get missed assignments and organize them by subject, making piles if need be. When your child is well enough, let him/her pick what to do first. If possible, get a "study buddy" who can call or e-mail daily about school and missed assignments. This way the sick student feels less socially isolated. If your child is sick—say with mononucleosis or pneumonia—you need to be assertive in asking for a reduced workload or Incomplete grade if needed. A child cannot recover from a long-term illness while doing make-up work and the current work when he returns to school.

Children with Emotional Difficulties

In my private practice I see children and teens with a broad spectrum of emotional issues. For example, some are children in foster or adoptive homes who have experienced abuse or neglect and have problems related to this trauma; others have bipolar disorder, anxiety, or other issues. Youth with emotional difficulties, whatever they may be and whatever their cause, often lack good homework habits. In these situations, parents should be very specific about their expectations for homework (i.e. time and place for completion) and the ways in which the child can obtain help from the parent. Homework clubs and after-school programs can be valuable resources, especially if other aspects of the parent-child relationship besides homework are contentious. Therapy may be needed to develop strategies to cope with negative behaviors.

Grandparents Raising Grandchildren

I see one unique challenge for the grandparent raising his or her grandchildren: length of time since completion of school. Depending on the age and health of the grandparent, dealing with homework problems can get out of hand, but I work with many healthy, energetic grandparents, too. Wisdom, good problem-solving skills, and patience are valuable currency in the homework wars, and many grandparents have plenty of each. It is helpful to be computer literate if you are raising your grandchildren. If you are not, seek help from family members, school, or other resources, either for learning to use a computer or for homework help with your grandchild.

Parents for Whom English is a Second Language

Having limited mastery of English can make it tough to be the homework coach. If possible, improve your mastery of English so that you can work with your children. If you have a relative or friend with better mastery of English, enlist their help with homework.

Use an after-school tutoring program or homework club if one is available. You can still teach your child study skills by using the study guide in 25 languages on www.studygs.net.

Homework Diagnostic #4 (see p. 88) offers a quick roundup of tips and techniques.

HOMEWORK DIAGNOSTICS #4: Coaches' Corner

General Tips

- ❏ Turn off TV, CD player, DVD player, pager, cell phone
- ❏ Stay calm
- ❏ Practice good stress management
- ❏ Divide your time wisely among siblings
- ❏ Work cooperatively with the other parent
- ❏ Avoid doing homework in the morning
- ❏ Have a sense of humor

Organizational Tips

- ❏ Break tasks down into smaller parts
- ❏ Plan your schedule for the afternoon/evening
- ❏ Make To-Do lists
- ❏ Examine your schedule and see if you have enough downtime
- ❏ Hire an organizing service
- ❏ Reward yourself

Homework in Two Homes

- ❏ Don't argue in front of the kids
- ❏ Come up with a homework plan that works with visitation schedule
- ❏ Designate one person to call the school, even if both of you attend meetings
- ❏ Copy school papers and report cards or read and send to the other parent

Single Parents or Parents with Chronic Illness

- ❏ Try to find a co-homework-coach, hopefully the other parent
- ❏ Use school-based or community-based tutoring programs
- ❏ Access support network of relatives, friends, clergy, school personnel

Parent of a Child With Chronic Illness

- ❏ Have good communication with the school
- ❏ Ask for a reduced workload
- ❏ Seek home-bound instruction as soon as possible
- ❏ If the child is well enough to do work, organize the makeup work and let the child pick what to do first
- ❏ Find a way for your child to keep in touch with a peer in the classroom

HOMEWORK DIAGNOSTICS #4: Coaches' Corner (cont.)

Parent of Child with Emotional Problems

❏ Consider how the emotional problem can affect homework completion

❏ Consider therapy

❏ Use homework clubs or after school tutoring programs, if necessary

Grandparents Raising Grandchildren

❏ If not computer literate, get help at library or in a class

❏ Develop supports in community, school, family and friends

Parent for Whom English is a Second Language

❏ Improve English skills

❏ Get help from relative or friend

❏ Use homework clubs or after-school tutoring

CHAPTER 8

The Homework Activist

I am often asked my opinion about whether children should have homework and how much homework is optimal for them. I believe there are clear pros and cons to homework, and I would like to tell you about them in this chapter. Nevertheless, the amount of homework your child is assigned depends on the teacher, the school, and the curriculum at that school. If you feel that the amount of homework is excessive, you may need to work to change school practices, but be forewarned: this can be an extremely lengthy process. In the meantime, you and your disorganized young person continue to be faced with homework daily, and if you are unlucky, on weekends and school vacations.

Parents Speak Out About Homework

Etta Kralovec and John Buell are educators and parents who challenge the notion of homework in their book, *The End of Homework* (Kralovec & Buell, 2000). Because you probably have math homework to check and may not have time to read it, the basis of the book is that in Blue Hill, Maine, in 1994, a committee consisting of members of the school board and community began meeting to address parents' concerns about excessive homework. The committee included Kralove and Buell, both parents as well as educators, who researched the pros and cons of homework, sparking a debate about balancing achievement and positive adjustment. This committee took a stand not only against homework in its community, but also the effects of homework on children and families everywhere. The committee speculated that children would not be well-rounded, well-adjusted individuals if they did homework almost to the exclusion of other activities.

Though the authors do not say that their efforts resulted in change in their community, their intent was to start a dialogue among educators and parents, and to provide a blueprint for homework activists. In short, they concluded that too much homework interferes with family functioning and development of the child in a myriad of ways. As educators, the reasoning behind the homework was clear, but in their opinion, flawed because the price is too high for families and children.

Achievement—At What Cost?

Teachers say that the reason that children and teenagers cannot get homework done is not because there is too much of it but because it is not always the highest priority: youth are in too many activities, watch excessive amounts of television, have part-time jobs, care for younger siblings, have two working parents and/or have personal problems (See Cooper [2001], for a detailed discussion of the educator perspective). Kralovec and Buell say that some teachers give a lot of homework to increase parental involvement. But do we want teachers deciding how we spend our spare time? They conclude that homework interferes with the parents' ability to decide how children should spend their time at home. In effect, they say, an excessive amount of homework impinges on the family unit.

Teachers also say that it is not easy to keep up with 150 or more students' homework, but that students achieve better when homework is assigned. Most of the pro-homework research, including that quoted by Kralovec and Buell, measures children's academic achievement in relation to homework. In my opinion, however, academic achievement is not the only measure of success. There is no measure of time lost playing outside, or stealing a few moments of watching cartoons or playing video games before bed after a long night of homework. No one measures the negative effects on parent-child relationships of the endless homework rat race, nor do they measure the effects of homework on self-esteem. I see many children who quit activities like Boy Scouts, sports, or music lessons because their homework takes up so much time. And how many times have we, as parents, had to miss or cancel a fun family activity due to homework? Is this fair to kids or parents? My clinical experience indicates that the emotional cost is quite high.

Is the Home Conducive to Homework?

Another issue is a thorny sociocultural one. The notion of homework as something done in a quiet, well-lit place with ample study materials and an adult at the child's disposal for guidance places many families at a disadvantage. Perhaps the parent isn't home from work until 6 or 7 P.M. Some students have religious practices that take up a substantial amount of time that teachers expect can be used for homework. Maybe the family lives in a small, noisy home with a large number of children and/or extended family members. Families may not have computers, live near a library, or have the money for a home reference library. One or both parents might have learning disabilities or mental disorders, or the family may be experiencing stressful life circumstances such as illness, job loss, or caring for grandparents. In any of these situations and others, students' ability to complete their homework is compromised. Dr. Harris Cooper, an educational expert, states that the amount of homework should depend on the "quality of support at home" and recommends that school homework policies "take into account the unique needs and circumstances of their students" (www.educationworld.com).

Burnout and Ideal Homework Levels

Many children have homework every weekend and school vacations over their academic careers. Some kids slug it out all summer, trying to get an edge up on the next grade. I spoke with a teenager recently who is reading all summer to get ready for AP English. Students in the class are given a summer reading list—summer homework—involving heavy hitters like Tolstoy, Dostoyevsky, and Bronte. Somehow, it doesn't seem right. When children have extraordinary amounts of homework, what can also occur is satiation, or loss of interest in school due to physical, emotional, and mental fatigue. Once a child stops caring about school, the road back to school success is long, indeed. Educational experts acknowledge that overloading children with homework, particularly in the elementary grades, can ruin motivation to be successful academically. This is why educational experts recommend 10 minutes per grade, so that first graders have ten minutes' homework, second graders have 20 minutes, and so on. If educators consistently followed these guidelines, the amount should be fine, but, of course, this doesn't always happen.

Leveling the Playing Field

In short, although homework certainly has benefits, too much homework may be too much of a good thing. Now, I am not anti-homework; it has never been my intention to start a homework revolution; what I want to do is to level the playing field for the average parent. As I finish writing about our journey, we have just had a four-day Spring break, and both of my high-school students had homework. They don't complain about it much; they know the drill. But it makes me angry that they had homework on vacation again. One of my middle-school-aged clients was working on three projects on his "vacation."

So how do we level the playing field when we are up against these odds? Try to have your children get the homework done at the very beginning or end of the vacation. That way the intervening days really are a vacation. I take them out for dinner at a favorite spot or someplace we have wanted to go but have not had time. On teacher inservice days, a party atmosphere pervades, if at all possible. If schools will not teach them to "work hard, play hard," then we will.

If you believe the amount of homework that your child has is truly excessive, consider organizing with other parents and the parent-teacher organization to approach the school board about homework practices and policies. This may be too much to ask of busy parents—I imagine than many parents would say that they are too busy making sure that the homework gets done to use precious time attending school board meetings—but if homework is really affecting your quality of life and your child's, it may be worth making the time to try and be a catalyst for change, and encouraging other parents to do the same.

CHAPTER 9

I Finished My Homework

Yes, you could hear these four words more often: I finished my homework. You could start having conversations after school like this:

You: "Hi, How was your day?"

Kid: "Fine."

You: "What's the homework situation?"

Kid: "Not bad."

It's true: if you persevere with these techniques, you'll find one day that homework will magically be completed while you do something else you *want* to do. Today, after many years of homework theatre (may your journey be much shorter), my disorganized son is achieving at his ability level in school—but even better, he is self-confident and happy. I no longer have constant contact with his teachers. I went to ninth grade open house, for once feeling like I did not have to troll for some type of data that might help us figure out why he wasn't doing well. As I write this, my son breezed by me and said, "I am organized." I smiled and said, "I know."

Other aspects of our lives have improved as homework has gotten easier, too. My underachieving son used to have a lot of trouble getting up in the morning; miraculously, as school and homework are under control, he gets up and goes through his morning routine without incident. His brother has become a skilled, patient tutor. We all have more free time. My husband and I are proud of our boys, but we are also proud that we toughed out this problem, got help when we needed it, and got beyond those nights that didn't go so well. Best of all, my son feels good that something positive has come out of his hard work in school.

To answer the question I asked at the start of the book: Whose homework is it? It felt like it was *our* homework for a long time. I meet a lot of parents who feel the same way. But once you get things under control and working smoothly, it becomes *your child's* homework with you in a supervising role.

It's not perfect, of course. I know that until both of my boys have graduated from high school (and college?), that homework headaches are a possibility. We have been coasting along with things going smoothly before, then something happens and we are in a Homework Hole. At least I now feel like I have some strategies under my belt to address them when they come up. And now, so do you.

Remember, however, that it took us a long time to get to this point, and it wasn't easy. In some ways, having a background in developmental and clinical psychology smoothed my path a bit. But in other ways, I am just like any other parent trying to raise children to the best of my ability. At times, I doubted myself and my family's ability to work through our homework troubles. Sometimes I felt like I couldn't take it anymore. Once, I picked up a newspaper, anxiously scanning an article with the headline, "ONE GUILTY IN HOMEWORK KILLING." (It actually read, "ONE GUILTY IN HOME*WOOD* KILLING.")

We had days where my son would come home and lie on the floor, distraught about his day at school, saying, "I hate that school.

I hate them all." My friends and family have been terrific supports in the homework war. As parents, we both spent a lot time worrying about the effects of homework on both our kids. We also worried that our disorganized young person would have trouble as an adult learning skills like paying bills on time, keeping track of house keys, and managing his money.

But, as I have worked to balance the demands of family, work and writing, my sons have had to do more chores. This morning, after they left for school, I found a neatly folded stack of pillowcases and towels, a testament to how far we have come. What 14-year-old boy stacks laundry neatly without specific instructions to do so? He is keeping a budget via computer, something we helped him to set up because he impulsively spends all his money. His room has some semblance of order; he washes and changes his own sheets, dusts and vacuums his room. Though he is too young for employment, he has a small babysitting business, specializing in playing video games with 6-to-11-year old boys. It makes me smile, then sigh, to think about all we have been through as a family. For years my disorganized son has been a good sport while his brother, friends, and classmates got academic awards. This week he received his first award for academic excellence at a school assembly. We would be just as proud of him if he had never trotted across the stage, feeling self-conscious, shaking hands with the teacher and principal. But there is some satisfaction in knowing that his teacher could see what we see: a bright young man who has to work harder than some kids at school.

The parent of the underachieving, disorganized child is relieved every time the homework gets done and when the good grades flow. We measure our children's accomplishments not in GPAs, AP courses, or SAT scores. We know that those barometers of scholarship do not guarantee success, though academic achievers get into better colleges. We know that success is also measured in hard work, character and the satisfaction of doing the best with what you've got. We know that doing well in school is important, but at the end of the day, we want a happy, well-adjusted child.

Respect your child's strengths, and practice good stress management. It will eventually get easier. In time, the homework drama at your house will become a distant memory.

CHAPTER 10

Resources For Students and Families

Ideas for Home Reference

Books

Unless otherwise indicated, all books are available through your local bookstore or through online booksellers.

Archer, A., & Gleason, M. (2002). *Skills for school success.* North Billerica, MA: Curriculum Associates, Inc. Great materials to use in third through sixth grade. Order them at 800/366-1158 or www.curriculumassociates.com

Didax Educational Resources. (2001). *Essential facts and tables.* Rowley, MA: Author. Available at www.worldteacherspress.com.

D. K. Publishing. (2002). *Ultimate visual dictionary.* New York: Author.

Great Source Education Group Staff. (2003). *Math on call.* Wilmington, MA: Great Source Education Group.

Pearce, Q. L. (2003). *Note taking and outlining: Grades 3–5.* Grand Rapids, MI: School Specialty Publishing. This and other titles in this series at www.schoolspecialtypublishing.com.

Pearce, Q. L. (2003). *Note taking and outlining: Grades 6–8,* Grand Rapids, MI: School Specialty Publishing. This and other titles in this series at www.schoolspecialtypublishing.com.

Suid, M. (1981). *Demonic mnemonics: Eight hundred spelling tricks for eight hundred tricky words.* Torrance, CA: Fearon Teacher Aids.

Zeman, A. & Kelly, K. (1997). *Everything you need to know about geography homework: A desk reference for students and parents—4th to 6th grades.* New York: Scholastic Inc. (See the rest of this series, as well: *Everything you need to know about American History, English, Math, Science,* and *World History homework.*)

Other Reference Materials

Quick study academic guides. Large array of laminated study guides are great for reference at home. English grammar and punctuation, mythology, periodic table of elements are a few examples of the guides. Order them at 800/230-9522 or www.quickstudy.com

Books About Homework for Kids

Berenstain, S. & Berenstain, J. (1997) *The Berenstain bears and the homework hassle.* New York: Random House. A charming book for young elementary school children. Brother Bear watches television, listens to music, and talks to friends on the phone instead of doing homework. This book attributes homework problems to laziness, however, so if your child has a learning or organizational problem, it may not be the best book for him or her.

Johnson D. & Johnson, C. (2002). *Homework heroes.* New York: Kaplan Books. For 6th to 8th graders who need a book on study strategies and key topics covered in middle school, this is a good choice. The very thorough chapter subheadings allow readers to look up information quickly and easily. Although it has no pictures or other devices to maintain interest, it is a good reference book for a reasonable price.

Lansky, B. (ed). (1997). *No more homework! No more tests! Kids' favorite funny school poems* (1997). Minnetonka, MN: Meadowbrook Press. I wish I'd found this book about 10 years earlier than I did. Humor and poetry—what a great way to manage homework stress! A fun book for a reasonable price ($8) with cool cartoon-like illustrations by Stephen Carpenter. For elementary and middle school-age children.

Nathan, A. (1996). *Surviving homework: Tips from teens that really work*. Brookfield, CT: The Millbrook Press. This book is the product of a questionnaire used by the writer with 300 high school students from all over the United States. It contains colorful cartoons throughout and ideas for solving common problems like writer's block, completing projects, and test anxiety. I liked this book a lot. Students who have well-established study skills or higher intellectual ability may feel the book talks down to them, however.

Romain, T. (1997). *How to do homework without throwing up*. Minneapolis, MN: Free Spirit Press. This humorous book with cartoons will interest even the most discouraged student. It has fun ways of conveying conventional homework wisdom, like "Homework has a speed limit. Do not write faster than 55 miles per hour." It covers common homework problems from a child's perspective.

Sebranek, P., Meyer, V., Kemper, D., & Van Rys, J. (1996). *School to work: A student handbook*. Lexington, MA: Write Source D.C. Heath and Co. This interesting book for high school or college students has many chapters pertaining to writing and applications of writing at work. Similarly, it talks about various ways to obtain information and how research is conducted in the work setting. There are tips for speaking, reading, and various other skills used in school and in work. The book contains mini-almanac in the back and nice table summarizing things like parts of speech, proofreading strategies, and so forth. The layout and graphics are appealing.

Books About Homework for Parents

Canter, *L. &* Hausner, *L. (1993). Homework without tears: A parent's guide for motivating children to do homework and to succeed in school.* New York: HarperResource. This book is written from an educator's perspective. It puts the onus of responsibility for school success on the parent, and I do not agree with that premise. It does contain some humorous cartoons and lots of checklists for the parent. Since this was published earlier than many of the others, you could probably get a used copy at a very reasonable price.

Cholden, H., Friedman, J., & Tiersky, E. (1998). *The homework handbook: Practical advice you can use tonight to help your child succeed tomorrow.* Chicago: Contemporary Books. This book talks about approaches that work for different types of students. Regardless of your child's "type," it is still the case that different strategies work for different children. This is one of the few books that touches on the emotional problems that can develop with the homework difficulties. I particularly liked the section "What Inhibits Learning" and the list of suggestions for teachers and administrators.

Cooper, H. (2001). *The battle over homework: Common ground for administrators, teachers, and parents.* Thousand Oaks, CA: Corwin Press, Inc. This book describes educational policy with regard to homework and reviews the existing research on aspects of homework. If you are trying to figure out why homework is necessary, this is the book you need to read. One caveat, however: it seems to be written more for educators than for parents.

Kralovec, E. & Buell, J. (2000) *The end of homework: How homework disrupts families, overburdens children, and limits learning.* Boston: Beacon Press. I mentioned this book in Chapter 8. The authors challenge traditional thinking about homework and posit that homework may not be beneficial to children or families. This book has a nice review of the history of homework.

Radencich, M. C. & Schumm, J. S. (1997). *How to help your child with homework: Every caring parent's guide to encouraging good study habits and ending homework wars.* Minneapolis, MN: Free Spirit Press. This book, for parents of children ages 6-13, has a lot of "how to's" like how to help your child read aloud, or how to improve your child's cursive writing. This is a nice resource if you need step-by-step direction, and if you, as a parent, have a lot of time to spend on the homework problem. Parents pressed for time will not like this book. It is a bit heavy on the parent role in homework and may not allow the child to work towards independent study habits.

Rosemond, J. (1990). *Ending the homework hassle: Understanding, preventing, and solving school performance problems.* Kansas City: Andrews and McMeel. This book has a couple of nice features. The chart on page 27 provides a self-assessment for the parent to determine whether he or she is overinvolved in homework versus being in a consulting role, for example. There is also a good chapter on common homework problems in Q&A format. The chapter entitled, "When to Medicate," gives a cogent discussion of the pros and cons of medication if your child is hyperactive. Keep in mind, however, that medications for ADHD have changed significantly this book was published in 1990.

Zentall, S.S. & Goldstein, S. (1998). *Seven steps to homework success: A family guide for solving common homework problems.* Plantation, FL: Specialty Press. This book confused me before I understood that the authors have developed something called the Learning Station, something that sounds like a tri-fold or presentation board used to cordon off a homework area for the child. Overall, this book seemed like way too much work for the parent, but I did like the authors' discussion of 11 common homework problems and possible solutions.

Internet Resources

For Students

www.aplusmath.com: This math website has free, printable flash-cards and homework help by topic. It also offers math games.

www.collegeboard.com: The College Board website provides valuable information on colleges and test preparation. You may not know that it contains free practice tests and an SAT Question of the Day. For a disorganized young person entering high school, this is a terrific way to plan ahead for the SAT so that the question formats and the scope of material on the test is familiar. This website also has a section on test-taking strategies.

www.ed.gov/pubs/parents/Homework: The U.S. Department of Education has a nice homework website. You can also access this information via http://k12s.phast.umass.edu.

www.factmonster.com: This website is broken down into fewer categories than some of the others. In particular, the study skills sections on writing essays or research papers are quite helpful.

www.funbrain.com: Has some math games that may be help your child. Various mathematical topics are covered in a fun way, like math baseball and "Mathcar racing" arcade-style math games.

www.homeworkspot.com: An array of resources separated by elementary, middle-school, and high-school grade levels and by subject. It has study breaks for each level that are links to puzzle or game sites. A parent resource page contains links to various topics relating to homework.

www.infoplease.com: I like the writing skills section of the Infoplease homework center. The site offers homework help by subject (Geography, History, Language Arts, Mathematics, Science, Social Studies). This website also has almanacs, an atlas, an encyclopedia, a dictionary, and a thesaurus.

www.kidsnet.org: This media guide search engine provides prompts to indicate title, grade level, curriculum area, and so forth.

www.libraryspot.com: Homework Spot's sister site, it contains reference materials on a wide range of topics.

www.lycoszone.com: If you get into the Lycos home page, it is easy to access an online encyclopedia, almanac, atlas, dictionary or foreign language translation program. Then it has website directories under different topics like geography or science.

www.math.com: Math help by topic, with unit quizzes. Uses pictures and graphics to maintain interest. The parent section, includes information on home schooling and special needs math students. Also contains a math glossary.

www.mathacademy.com: Has a good article on math anxiety and other features.

www.multnomah.lib.or.us/lib/homework/index.html: The librarians at Multnomah County, Oregon Multinomah Homework Center developed this incredible website for research on the web.

www.nationalgeographic.com: For a reluctant learner having trouble in science, this website is a goldmine. It has homework help under six topics: animals, history/culture, maps/geography, photos/art, places, and science/nature. It also has a list of science links.

www.refdesk.com: This one has a really comprehensive list of homework help on the Internet by subject and there is a brief description of these websites. It is divided by grades 1st to 6th, 7th and 8th, 9th to 12th, and college.

www.school.discovery.com: B.J. Pinchbeck's Homework Helper (now part of DiscoverySchool.com) This website can connect your child with many other websites by topic. I especially like the Puzzlemaker feature, where you can turn something you are studying into a game with crossword puzzles or word searches. It also has some neat games, like 10 adventures that take the student around the world.

www.studygs.net: This Study Guides Strategy website has a comprehensive study guide that can be downloaded in 25 languages. It is a great resource for students for whom English is a second language, as well as a fun website for students taking a foreign language.

www.ucc.vt.edu/studysk/checklis.html: The Virginia Tech, Division of Student Affairs website has a handy study skill checklist if you need help defining the problems as either time scheduling, concentration, listening and note taking, reading, exams, or writing skills. Most applicable to college and high school students.

For Parents

www.abledev.com: Glossary of mental health terms.

www.apa.org: Website of the American Psychological Association.

www.askdrmath.com: Offers math resources by subject, including college to advanced mathematics. Answers all kinds of math questions. A good website for the parent who is having trouble helping the student with math.

www.educationworld.com: This website, which calls itself "The Educator's Best Friend," contains articles about homework from the educator's perspective.

www.familyeducation.com: Has a variety of resources, including an e-mail newsletter for parents. It has information divided by Pre-K to 2nd grade, 3rd to 5th, and 6th to 12th grade. For example, there is an article with step-by-step directions on how to help your child with multiplication quizzes and spelling tests. For $20, the Homework Relief Center offers printable lessons by grade level. This seems like a terrific resource with children who forget to bring home their books. I also like the section "50 Fun Ways to Improve Reading."

www.help4adhd.org: This website has various information pertaining to ADHD in children and adults, but I like the "Dealing With

Systems" sections and the one called "Organizing the Home and Office." You can also call 800/233-4050 for assistance.

www.nea.org: National Education Association webpage that features help for parents such as "A parent's guide to helping children learn to read."

www.neuropsychologycentral.com: Good resources pertaining to neuropsychology.

www.nimh.gov: Website of the National Institutes of Mental Health.

www.schwablearning.org: This website contains a parent's guide to help children with learning difficulties. Even if your child does not have ADHD or a learning disability, this is a great resource. There is a great section on test-taking strategies including true-false, multiple choice, open book, fill-in-the-blank, matching, and essay. Study strategies like using mnemonics and memorization tips are included. I also like their list of "20 tips to promote self-esteem."

www.search.about.com: The about.com website has a topical guide for links such as quotations by topic. Although this can be a great homework resource, this is a website for adults, so it lacks the kid-friendly features of some of the others.

Videos

Homework? I'll do it later! Boys Town, NE: Boys Town Press. Available for sale at 800/282-6657 or www.boystownpress.org.

Study strategies made easy: A practical plan for school success—Grades 6-12. Plantation, FL: Specialty Press, Inc. Available for sale at 800/233-9273 or www.addwarehouse.com.

Schoolhouse rock: Multiplication rock, Grammar rock, America rock, Money rock, Science rock. Disney Studios.

References

American Psychiatric Association. (1994). *Diagnostic and statistical manual of mental disorders* (4th ed.). Washington, DC: Author.

Barkley, Russell A. (1998). *Attention-deficit hyperactivity disorder: A handbook for diagnosis and treatment* (2nd ed). New York: The Guilford Press.

Barkley, Russell A. (2000*). Taking charge of ADHD*. New York: The Guilford Press.

Barnett, R. C. & Greis, K. D. (2004) *Community, family, and work program: Parental After-school stress project—Report of findings, April 8, 2004*. Retrieved May 27, 2005, from http://www.nsba.org/site/pdf.asp?TP=/site/docs/34200/34110.pdf

Chrysler, W. (1957). *Life of an American Workman*. The Curtis Publishing Co.

Denckla, M. B. and Reader, M. J. (1993) Education and psychosocial interventions: Executive dysfunction and its consequences. In R. Kurlan, (Ed.), *Handbook of Tourette syndrome and related tic and behavioral disorders (*pp. 431–451). Rochester, NY: Marcel Decker, Inc.,

Denckla, M. B. (1996). A theory and model of executive function: A neuropsychological perspective. In G. Reid Lyon & Normal A. Krasnegor (Eds.), *Attention, memory, and executive function* (pp. 263–277). Baltimore: Paul H. Brookes.

Ellenberg, L. (1999). Executive functions in children with learning disabilities and attention deficit disorder. In J. A. Incorvaia, B. S. Mark-Goldstein, and D. Tessmer, (Eds.), *Understanding, diagnosing, and treating AD/HD in children and adolescents* (pp. 197–219). Northvale, NJ: Jason Aaronson, Inc.

Lite, L. (1996). *The Children's Relaxation Book*. Plantation, Florida: Specialty Press, Inc.

Prentice Hall Online Textbooks. Retrieved May 27, 2005 from http://phschool.com/successnet/teacher_center/home.html.

Thayer, E. & Zimmerman, J. (2001). *The Co-parenting Survival Guide*. Oakland, CA: New Harbinger Press.

Wender, H. (2002). *ADHD: Attention-deficit/hyperactivity disorder in children and adolescents*. London: Oxford University Press.

Wilens, T. E. (1999). *Straight talk about psychiatric medications for kids*. New York: The Guilford Press.

About the Author

Sally G. Hoyle, PhD, is a licensed psychologist who received her doctoral degree in Clinical Psychology from The Ohio State University.

Dr. Hoyle specializes in the treatment of abused children, adolescents, and families in crisis. She also works with children who display disruptive behaviors, social skills deficits, adjustment, and school problems.

Dr. Hoyle also gives workshops to parents and professionals on child development and parenting. Her previous books published by CWLA Press include, *When Do I Go Home? Intervention Strategies for Foster Parents and Helping Professionals and The Sexualized Child in Foster Care: A Guide for Foster Parents and Professionals.* She works in private practice in Pittsburgh, PA.